GIFT OF

PAN AMERICAN ROUND TABLE

II

Mars Moves South

MARS MOVES SOUTH:
The
Future Wars
of
South America

by
NORMAN D. ARBAIZA

An Exposition-University Book
EXPOSITION PRESS   JERICHO, NEW YORK

FIRST EDITION

© 1974 by Noman D. Arbaiza

Library of Congress Catalog Card Number: 73-92847

ISBN 0-682-47897-0

Manufactured in the United States of America

For Gertrude

Contents

Mars Moves South

ONE

The Hypothesis and the Question

The first hypothesis is that the technologically advanced nations of the world will, for a variety of reasons (see Chapter Two), tend during the last quarter of the twentieth century to abandon the practice of creating and maintaining empires: in other words they will tend toward exerting less and less effort to control the less technologically advanced nations.

A second hypothesis is that, if the validity of the first is substantiated by the events of the next two or three decades, then the technologically backward nations will take to warring among themselves; they will fight among themselves, for a variety of compelling reasons.

The question is: what wars can we foresee in South America?

TWO

The Declining Profitability of Empire

The third quarter of the twentieth century has been a time during which the profitability of maintaining an empire has sharply declined. Perhaps the most dramatic example is Indo-China, into which first the French and then the Americans on one side, and the Russians on the other, have poured huge quantities of matériel and money, and in the case of the first two, men, without being able to show the taxpayer any profit at all. Less sensational but probably equally costly has been the maintenance by the Soviet Union and the United States of idle armies staring at each other on the European continent for a quarter of a century. In these two cases the taxpayer, though not shown a profit, has been at least partially lulled into acceptance by propaganda describing a death struggle between communism and capitalism; but it seems that as the century's third quarter draws to a close, so is the taxpayer's acceptance of the propaganda coming to an end.

In other areas the struggle to maintain or create empires (primarily but not solely between the United States and the Soviet Union) has grown both more costly and more pointless. The United States has poured thousands of millions of dollars into Latin America, has sent in its own troops and financed mercenary armies; but with all this, Latin America has not become an exclusively American market, American companies operating in Latin America have not become inviolate, the Caribbean has not been made an American lake; nor has capitalism become a more vital force in the minds of all Latin Americans than socialism. The attaining of any one, or all, of the foregoing goals would have been a victory for U.S. foreign policy and a possible justification of empire-building in Latin

5

America; the complete failure of this policy to achieve *any* of its goals not only suggests that the techniques of empire-building were poorly conceived and badly executed, but also opens up the possibility that the whole concept of empire belongs to the past (and perhaps to the future) and is unnecessary, imprudent, and counterproductive among developed nations in the final quarter of this century.

This hypothesis is strengthened by the fact that those technologically advanced nations which emerged from World War II bereft of any vestige of empire, and which made no attempt to regain old empires or create new ones, have prospered mightily (West Germany and Japan). Other nations which never had an empire and have not tried to create one have also prospered (Scandinavia). France has only begun to prosper after abandoning her post-war attempts to recoup or retain its empire in Indo-China and Africa. The Soviet Union, which built a post-war empire (the Baltic states, Poland, Czechoslovakia, East Germany and the Balkans), has notably lagged in internal economic development, which has not been aided either by outpourings of money, men, and matériel to Indo-China, Cuba, the Arab states and other areas where it has contested U.S. control of client states. The United States prospered in the immediate post-war period, when it was the only source of manufactured goods left intact, but as the other nations rebuilt themselves, the American economy has begun to falter badly, and has proven itself unable to compete with other advanced nations, particularly with those which, like West Germany and Japan, have declined to assume what is today the needless burden of empire. The outpouring of money from the U.S., the maintenance abroad of costly bases, armies, and fleets, and the prosecution of profitless wars, have diverted to foreign lands and peoples capital which ought to have been used to modernize, renew, and add to the nation's industrial plant so as to make it competitive with German and Japanese industry.

But other factors tending to reduce the usefulness of empires to today's technologically advanced nations exist, and may in the long run be even more compelling reasons than those suggested above for abandoning the entire empire concept during the century's last quarter. The world's great post-Napoleonic empires (and incidentally the term "empire" is used to include spheres of influence such as Central America vis-à-vis the United States as well as outright territories and possessions such as Puerto Rico) were the British, the French, and the American, and their purpose was to insure a supply of certain raw materials, to provide a marketplace for manufactured goods, and to provide sites for military and naval bases to put down native uprisings, keep the sealanes open, and keep other empire-builders out.

The early phases of the creation of the American empire are sometimes mistakenly seen as internal matters since the conquered territories were contiguous to the metropole, which can be defined as being made up at first by the thirteen colonies. The Louisiana Purchase (1803), the accession of Florida (1819), the accession of Texas, New Mexico, Arizona, California, Nevada, Utah and part of Colorado and the organization of Oregon (1848) were all classic empire-building. The Civil War (1861-1865) can be seen as an attempt by the metropole (here defined as Boston/New York) to retain the South as a supplier of raw materials (cotton) and a marketplace for manufactured goods (machinery, textiles). Although contiguity may mask the empire effect, all these matters involved competition with other empires, notably the British, French, and Spanish, and with Mexico. Other aggrandizement of the American empire, either by military conquest or economic control, would include the Caribbean, Panama, the Philippines, Hawaii, other Pacific islands, Central America, and, after World War II, attempts to secure control of South America, parts of Africa and Asia, etc.

Be that as it may, the tremendous forward strides of post-World War II technology are tending to make control of sources of raw materials less and less necessary (synthetic nitrate instead of Chilean saltpeter, nylon rope instead of Manila fiber, synthetic instead of natural rubber, and so on). If we look forward not too many years, may we not see cheap power produced by atomic power plants running the factories and powering automobiles using rechargeable electric batteries? The effect of this on the economies of the oil-producing countries of North Africa and South America is horrendous to contemplate. Even without technology, the oil-buyers' league consisting of Europe, Japan and the U.S., proposed in 1973, would bring the oil-producing nations to heel. Also, if Australia, New Zealand and Canada are included among the advanced nations of the world, the technologically developed world can feed itself and has no need to import food from the backward nations, except perhaps a luxury crop or two such as coffee. At the same time, purchasing power in the advanced nations is so much greater than in the backward ones that the latter are tending to lose their value as present or potential mass markets for sophisticated non-military equipment; however, their technologists are not so backward that they cannot supply themselves with the ordinary manufactured items of day-to-day consumption such as textiles and preserved food. Will the advanced nations of the world which are still empire-oriented (the U.S.S.R. and the U.S. particularly) long continue to deplete themselves and lose ground to their rivals (Europe and Japan) in order to control countries the domination of which brings only economic drain and no profit? It seems unlikely that the Russian and American taxpayers will allow this to continue.

The only seemingly realistic reason for continuing to try to control the backward nations is fear; that is to say, the advanced nations may feel that if the backward nations are not controlled, they may attack the developed world. However, if the developed world is allied and busily trading within itself, and maintains its technological advancement, such a fear must be groundless. While it is true that the U.S. in a sense lost a war in Indo-China, it was never itself endangered.

If, then, we can hypothesize that the trend during the final quarter of the twentieth century is to be one of less and less concern or interference on the part of the advanced nations into the technologically underdeveloped areas of the world, what will happen in *those* areas? In particular, insofar as this inquiry is concerned, what will happen to the nations of South America? As the advanced nations outgrow wars and the need for empire, will the nations of South America seek to form their own empires, and wage their own wars? Will this be their only way of themselves becoming advanced? Will Mars, the god of war, move south?

THREE

The Gifts of History

If war is viewed as a desirable end, and we believe it will be so viewed by more than one South American government as the advanced nations become less and less concerned with that continent, then it will be needful to find convincing reasons for whatever particular martial adventure is being contemplated. This is an ancient art, but to be successfully practiced the reasons set forth must never be frivolous or spurious, but must be seen by the people as serious and legitimate. National anthems and waving flags, marching bands, propaganda and patriotism will heighten public enthusiasm only if the people perceive serious and legitimate reasons for the desired war. We need look no further than Vietnam to see a glaringly clear example of popular rejection (by both the American and the South Vietnamese people) of a war undertaken for what were seen to be spurious reasons, despite years of propaganda.

There are many sorts of acceptable reasons for war that can be used. Self-defense, the righting of past wrongs, the promise of future advantage, the superiority of one race or religion over another are some of the most common. The waging of war in order to bring benefits such as democracy to the enemy or to the whole world, although used by the United States, tends to be a flabby reason; students of World War II will remember that the declaration of war against Germany, then seen by Roosevelt as the main enemy, had to be held up despite years of anti-Nazi propaganda until Japan physically attacked the United States; this created a legitimate popular casus belli and the war against Germany was slipped in through the back door, as it were.

In any event, some of these legitimate causes of war grow out of an immediate circumstance, a new situation, but some are

11

historical hangovers: some past treaty, claim, or accident may have left a nation in a position that can by efficient propaganda be exploited as a reason for war. Such reasons are seen by would-be warmakers as gifts of history, and in this chapter we want to look at a few of them in South America.

The decision to limit this inquiry to South America, rather than extend it to include all of what is loosely called "Latin America," is based on two factors. First, South America is a clearly defined geographic area but at the same time the term includes no implications of homogeneity of peoples or cultures, while the broader term "Latin America" has come to imply some sort of unity or common purpose, as for instance in the expression "the Latin American vote in the United Nations" or "the Latin American point of view" or "relations between the United States and Latin America." This, like the use of terms such as "the free world," "the communist bloc," "the third world," has become a convention, but these are dangerous conventions because the convenience of using them may beguile both writer and reader alike into believing that such entities truly exist, where in fact they may have only a tenuous existence, or none at all.

The other reason for limiting this study to the nations of South America is that the nations of northern Latin America have, to a great or lesser degree, and with the possible exception of Mexico, never really been independent at all, but have been either wholly or partially part of either the Spanish or the American empire, de facto or de jure, and thus must properly be studied separately, and not linked with South America under the general term "Latin America."

In examining these "gifts of history" or potential South American trouble spots, we shall start as far to the south as one can go, and then work our way north through South America.

A. THE WEDDELL QUADRANT

Our first potential trouble spot may seem far-fetched; it seems hardly credible that men might fight over an expanse of seemingly useless ice, or go to the trouble and expense of sending expeditions there, and maintaining weather stations in an icy wilderness, just to establish a claim to something which seems to have no value. But aside from the demonstrable fact that mankind has proven itself willing to fight over almost anything, there are aspects of Antarctica that are often overlooked. In the first place, the land under the ice is a continent of 5,300,000 square miles (compared with 6,800,000 square miles for all of South America); if the glacial ice that covers it were to melt, the sea level would rise 200 feet and drown the coastal civilizations of the world, and incidentally convert the Amazon basin into an inland sea (Manaus, Brazil, is only 160 feet above present sea level). The ice cover is often two miles thick, and the state of the art today does not permit reaching the land underneath for any wealth that may be there, but the rapid strides of twentieth-century technology may make that possible (without melting the ice) sooner than one imagines, so that the "claims" of Chile, Argentina, and Brazil may not, after all, be as ridiculous as they might have seemed at first glance.

The antarctic regions are generally thought of as being that part of the earth's surface enclosed within the 60th south parallel; this area, if viewed on a flat projection, will be seen to be a great circle, with the south pole as its center (see Map A). This circle has been sliced into four equal sections, or quadrants, as one might slice a pie. The section that lies between zero degrees (the Greenwich meridian) and 90 degrees west longitude is known as the Weddell quadrant (after a British explorer), and it is into this quadrant that the southern tip of South America almost intrudes. A goodly portion of the Weddell quadrant (that part of it between 20 and 80 degrees west longitude) is conventionally called the Falkland Island Dependencies (FIDS), and there exists some sort of presumption or claim that whoever owns the Falkland Islands also owns that portion of Antarctica; both Great Britain and Argentina claim ownership of the Falkland Islands (called the Islas Malvinas by the Argentines), and the claim to the so-called dependencies is probably more important than the claim to the islands themselves. Both Argentina and Great Britain buttress their claims by expeditions and weather stations. However, Chile, which makes no claim to the

MAP A

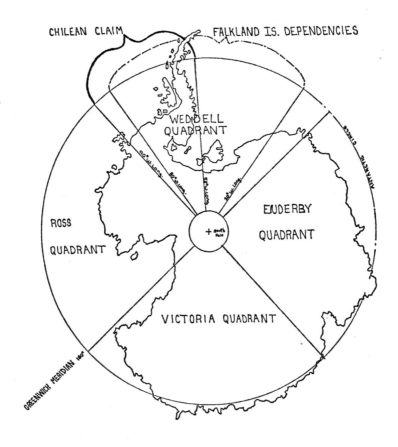

Map drawn by Rosario Calabrese.

islands, also claims a slice of Weddell's quadrant, namely that between 53 and 90 degrees west longitude, and also maintains a presence. A new presence in the quadrant will be Brazil's, and a Brazilian newspaper (*Journal da Tarde* of São Paulo) has written of a "diplomatic offensive by the Brazilian government [aimed at] taking possession of the antarctic territory to which it has a right." A Brazilian antarctic expedition is planned for the seventies.

A 1959 treaty signed in Washington reserves the antarctic regions for scientific research for 30 years (until 1989) and purports to set aside all national territorial claims until that time. To what extent, if at all, Argentina and Chile will be bound by this treaty remains to be seen. Brazil protested not having been included in the negotiations that led up to it, but this "protest," made in 1964, seems to actually have been the institution of a claim.

In any event, the news of any technological breakthrough that might make the Weddell quadrant in any way exploitable would immediately set off a three-way struggle (not necessarily armed) among Argentina, Brazil, and Chile, with the United States, until 1989 at least, presumably adopting a "hands-off" position, and Britain involved in some way, which qualifies the quadrant as at least a potential trouble spot. Even without a scientific breakthrough, a power struggle between, say, Argentina and Chile, or Brazil and Argentina, or Brazil and Spanish-speaking America, would find in Weddell's quadrant an additional bone of contention.

B. ARGENTINA AND CHILE

Moving northward from Antarctica, we find that there have been repeated border disputes between these two southernmost nations, some in the north but mostly in the south. These were supposed to have been settled in 1902, and the settlement was commemorated by the building of the Christ of the Andes, a gigantic statue. In the last few years, the disputes have mostly centered around Tierra del Fuego and some tiny islands in the Beagle Channel far to the south; the undisputed possession of these islands by either nation would eventually tend to strengthen that country's claim to all or part of the Falkland Island Dependencies (see foregoing section on Weddell's Quadrant) and to certain oil deposits. However, a more serious potential bone of contention between Argentina and Chile is the presence of great numbers of Chileans in southern Argentina. The commander of the frontier division of Argentina's national police, Amadeo Parea, said in 1966 that "we may well consider our southland occupied by a foreign country." A similar situation between El Salvador and Honduras did in fact lead to sharp fighting, and might also in Patagonia or Tierra del Fuego, should the Chileans seem to be "taking over," or should Argentina adopt strong measures to control or expel them. Possibly with this in mind, Argentina adopted a law in 1967 providing that all *residents* over 14 years of age may be drafted when "interests vital to the integrity of the state are seen to be threatened, interfered with, or substantially perturbed and it becomes necessary to preserve internal order." Foreigners can refuse to be drafted but by so doing they renounce their right to reside in Argentina.

Any attempt by Argentina to draft large groups of Chilean men, women, and teen-agers, or failing that, to expel them forcibly from places where they have lived for years, might easily provoke a nasty situation and provide grist for the propaganda mills on both sides of the Andes. The seriousness of the situation may be seen in the fact that at least 42% of the population of Patagonia and Tierra del Fuego is composed of Chileans. The situation is not as bad in the rest of the country, except in Jujuy Province in the north, but it is estimated that over 1,100,000 foreigners reside in Argentina, mostly Chileans, Paraguayans, and Bolivians, and mostly employed in menial jobs. The character of the Chilean population resident in Argentina is tending to broaden, however, with the flight of tens of thousands of middle-class Chilean families to Argentina, fleeing the socialist government in Chile. These middle-class immigrants, if they remain despite Allende's overthrow, may be seen by the Argentine middle class as even more of a threat than their working-class predecessors.

Should Argentina enter into a period of severe economic crisis, the presence of a large number of job-seeking or employed foreigners competing with Argentines who are out of work could easily contribute to xenophobia; if the foreigners were forced out of jobs and onto some kind of relief or welfare, and become a tax burden, the situation could be worsened. If they were forced out of Argentina and back into Chile, Bolivia, and Paraguay, the mood might become even uglier on both sides. Already lands are said to have been set aside by the Argentine governor of Tierra del Fuego as internment camps for Chileans.

C. CHILE'S NORTHWARD PUSH

The War of the Pacific (1879-1882) was an expansionist move by Chile, aimed at annexing the nitrate-rich deserts of what is now northern Chile, but was, prior to the war, southern Peru (Tarapacá) and Bolivia's only seacoast (Antofagasta). Chile's numbing victory over the combined forces of Peru and Bolivia created scars which have not yet healed. The memory of the humiliating defeat still rankles the Peruvian military; also, the drawn-out nature of the settlement, which was not complete until 1929, 47 years after the end of hostilities, has tended to fuel the flames of resentment and keep the arms race going.

A few months before assuming the presidency of Peru in a coup d'état in October 1968, General Velasco denied having said that he feared a Chilean attack aimed at taking possession of a copper mine in southern Peru; Dr. Allende, the socialist President of Chile, has stated that Latin American countries, because of their common origin and tragedy of underdevelopment, should seek other ways than confrontation to resolve their differences. Nevertheless, both men, when presidents of their respective countries and both trying to lead their countries toward socialism, did not stop the arms race. Allende's overthrow and the new rightist government in Chile can only heighten the tension. Chile had had two frigates and two submarines built in Britain, has bought a cruiser from Sweden (the *Latorre*) to add to the two cruisers it already had (the *O'Higgins* and the *Pratt*), has obtained one C-130 transport aircraft and paratrooper equipment from the U.S. as well as an armed fleet tug and a landing craft. Peru's purchase of twelve French Mirage jets is explained

by Peru's leading daily newspaper *El Comercio* as "reestablish-
ing the balance broken by the recent acquisitions made by Chile
without justifiable motive." In March 1970 Peru also bought
Canadian De Haviland Buffalo planes and planned to buy U.S.
Hercules transports and, in 1972, SA-16 Albatross planes and
more helicopters; two new destroyers (the *Ferré* and the *Pal-
acios*) were scheduled to be received during 1973 from England
for Peru's navy, as well as a Dutch cruiser, the *Grau*. Jet planes
and cruisers are not what is needed to put down insurgents nor
yet to catch U.S. tuna clippers illegally fishing in territorial
waters; nor did the common bonds of socialism and anti-U.S.
feelings prove to be a balm to Chilean-Peruvian relations.

Another scar left over from the War of the Pacific is Chile's
continued occupation of Antofagasta, Bolivia's only exit to the
sea, which not only damages pride but also frustrates trade. One-
time President Barrientos of Bolivia has said that access to the
sea is a matter of life and death for Bolivia. A later president,
Ovando, denied accusations by a Chilean senator (Bulnes) to
the effect that Bolivia was planning to invade Chile and recapture Antofagasta, but a still later president (of whom Bolivia
has had 185 in 146 years of existence) was shopping for jets in
Spain in 1972. Chilean-Bolivian diplomatic relations have been
broken since 1962, but the theme of an outlet to the Pacific has
been common to all of Bolivia's regimes, whether rightist, leftist,
or whatever. In 1966 Barrientos threatened not to attend the
summit meeting of hemisphere presidents unless this matter
was placed on the agenda. The possibility of a new sort of
rapprochement was introduced by Bolivian president Banzer's
reported willingness (1972) to resume ties with Chile if Chile
would grant access to the sea in return for "non-territorial geographic" concessions on the part of Bolivia; while not spelt out,
these were presumed to mean diversion of sweet water from
Bolivian rivers, or petroluem, or some such quid pro quo.

Bolivia is itself perhaps a potential casus belli, as will be
seen later, but for the moment looking only at the Chilean-
Bolivian-Peruvian situation, it will be seen that the matter of
egress to the sea has assumed immediate importance because
of the oil strikes in the Santa Cruz region of Bolivia in 1966;

the trans-Andean pipeline to Arica (Chile) may be insufficient and could be closed by Chile; an alternate route through Ilo or Matarani could be closed by Peru. What probably amounts to six trillion cubic feet of natural gas is also lying underground in Santa Cruz awaiting some sort of egress, as well as hundreds of millions of barrels of crude. Meanwhile, to the east of Santa Cruz lies Brazil, consuming three times as much oil as it produces; the difference could be cut by Bolivian oil. Most of the oil that does flow from Bolivia to the Pacific is destined for the west coast of the U.S., but Peru has also initiated purchases of Bolivian crude (1971), and Argentina and Brazil are also interested. As we shall see also in following sections, the question of "whither Bolivian gas and crude" is indeed a very live issue, and may involve Bolivia's destiny.

D. THE ACCIDENTAL COUNTRIES

Until 1776 Charcas (now Bolivia but then known also as High Peru or Alto Perú) was governed by an *audencia* (a body with certain legislative, executive, and judicial functions) which in theory at least was responsible to the Spanish Viceroy in Lima; in that year the Viceroyalty of La Plata was created with its seat of government in Buenos Aires, and Bolivia was transferred to it. La Plata at about that time included all of what is now Argentina, Uruguay and Paraguay, as well as Bolivia. Thus, as the end of the eighteenth century (and of the Spanish Empire) approached, South America consisted of three Spanish viceroyalties: La Plata, as described above, Peru (including Chile), and New Granada (Ecuador, Panama, Colombia, and Venezuela). The English, French, and Dutch had relatively small possessions in the Guianas, and the Portuguese viceroyalty of Brazil, then as now, occupied the rest of the continent, per the Spanish-Portuguese treaty of Ildefonso (1777).

The three Spanish viceroyalties were to fragment into nine independent but weak nations (later ten when Panama became independent of Colombia, although for all practical purposes a dependency of the United States). This splitting-up process, blamed by many historians for Spanish-speaking South America's military and economic weakness, instability and "underdevelop-

ment," had many roots. It is of course idle to speculate what
might have been Spanish South America's history during the
past 150 years if it had been divided into three strong countries
instead of nine weak ones. Future alliances, customs unions
and wars of conquest may attempt to reestablish something of
the sort, and we shall be looking at those possibilities later. For
the moment, we would like to consider some of the causes for the
fragmentation of the viceroyalties. One common factor was that
no one of the Spanish viceroyalties (including New Spain or
what is today Mexico and Central America) was ever truly a
single entity; there always existed interior political divisions,
called *audiencias* or captaincies-general or *presidencias* or *gobernaciones,* which tended to retain their form and autonomy after
independence from Spain. The colonial period during which the
sense of identity took hold had lasted, after all, from two to
three centuries. More important, perhaps, is the fact that it was
to the advantage of the local creole aristocracy to control its
own territory ("creole" used here in the sense of a white person
born in the New World). After all, one of the main reasons for
desiring independence from Spain was the resentment on the
part of the creoles of the fact that the "peninsulars" (i.e., white
people sent from Spain, generally with high office) got all the
good appointments. Thus, a white native-born Chilean aristocrat
would hardly want to exchange subordination to someone from
Lima for subordination to someone from Spain. On a very practical basis, the fact that Bolivia, Paraguay, Uruguay, and Argentina are all independent today instead of united, creates duplica-
tion in that it requires four armies, four navies, four airforces,
four diplomatic services, four government structures, etc., but
it also creates more jobs for generals, admirals, presidents, am-
bassadors, governors, etc., all of whom have been until recently
traditionally drawn from the white creole aristocracy.

However, in the specific cases of the three "accidental" nations we are now considering (Bolivia, Paraguay and Uruguay)
there are other special reasons that brought about their independence, in addition to the general reasons listed above.

Bolivia. The transfer of Charcas to La Plata in 1776 in no
way settled the matter of the ownership of the area. In the early

days of independence both Peru and Bolivia feared that Simón Bolívar would try to absorb them into Gran Colombia (now Ecuador, Colombia and Venezuela), despite a proclamation of Bolivian independence made at Chuquisaca (now Sucre) in 1825, where the country's name was also changed, lending credence to the cynics who say that Bolivia exists because Bolívar wanted a country named after him. In any event the Peruvians under Gamarra invaded Bolivia and drove out Bolívar's general Sucre and the Colombian forces under his command. Another general, Santa Cruz, was elected president. Both Gamarra and Santa Cruz appeared to favor union of the two countries, but the question arose as to which influence (Peruvian creole or Bolivian mestizo) would predominate. Political chaos in Peru (where Gamarra had been fighting Orbegoso for mastery) allowed Santa Cruz to invade and defeat the Peruvian forces under Salaverry, who had been proclaimed military dictator for the time. This same Salaverry, perhaps foreseeing the future rivalry between Chile and Peru, had attempted to initiate a sort of customs union between them, possibly as a wedge against Chilean intervention in an eventual Peruvian-Bolivian federation. Santa Cruz, however, defeated Salaverry and proclaimed, under his rule, the Confederación Perú-Boliviana. Neither Chile nor Argentina wanted to see the establishment of a strong state on their borders, and sent armies to break up the confederation, which was done (1839) and Santa Cruz was compelled to leave the country. Now Gamarra, back in power in Peru, invaded Bolivia but without success; he was killed in battle and Chile again intervened, this time as mediator, and the two nations became from then on (1841) separate entities, although they were destined to again fight together against Chile, and to be again defeated by Chile (1879-1882, see "Chile's Northward Push" above). Thus, it may be said that Bolivia's existence as an independent entity is a result of Chile's and Argentina's unwillingness to see a Peruvian-Bolivian union, as well a result of internal struggles within Peru and Bolivia themselves. Bolívar, whose name is anathema in southern South America, is assigned the blame by various sources, and while it is probably true that it was his influence that kept Bolivia out of a possible La Plata confederation in the first place (conference of Chuquisaca, 1825), it must be remembered that he was in disgrace and dead by 1830. As a matter of fact, had San Martín obtained the ascendency over Bolívar, instead of the other way around, Bolivia would probably have been given to Argentina, or been divided among Argentina, Chile and Peru, and not have existed at all. As it is, however, it does exist and is a potential trouble spot from several directions.

This tug of war among Chile, Peru and Argentina, with Bolivia as the rope, has generally had to do with the western, or mountainous, region of Bolivia. The eastern part of Bolivia (consisting of the provinces of Pando, Beni and Santa Cruz) has been the subject of dispute with Bolivia's other neighbors, Paraguay and Brazil. Santa Cruz attempted to secede from Bolivia and become part of Brazil in 1924. Before that, Bolivia lost a slice of what is now Brazilian Redônia (1867), and in 1904 lost the whole of the province of Acre to Brazil. Today, considerable areas of the Bolivian Amazon region are populated largely by Brazilians.

The bloody Chaco war between Bolivia and Paraguay, which started in 1927 and wasn't finally settled until 1938, ended with Bolivia giving up claims to over 100,000 square miles of the Gran Chaco region. This constitutes a third of the Gran Chaco, an enormous plain 600 to 800 feet above sea level, alternately covered by jungle, open woodland, marshes and grassy plains, and comprising a sort of interior heartland of Bolivia, Paraguay and Argentina. At present mainly valuable for its quebracho, used for tanning leather, and possibilities for future exploitation are great, even if oil is not found. The possibility of making the shallow rivers navigable with hovercraft or hydrofoils, especially the Pilcomayo and Bermejo, or road construction, could open the area to the sea via the Paraná to Buenos Aires.

In any case, pieces of Bolivia have been hacked away (Antofagasta, Rondônia, Acre, the Chaco) and the possibility remains that the process will continue. Its extreme political, military and economic weakness, combined with its potential richness, makes it an attractive target for dismemberment.

Paraguay. Paraguay's struggle for existence began well before independence, when the King of Spain (Ferdinand VI), ceded part of Paraguay to Portugal (1750); this was resisted by the Paraguayan Jesuits, who early demonstrated the fighting capacities of this little landlocked country where machismo seems inborn. It took the combined forces of Spain and Portugal to defeat the Paraguayans. The victors then disputed the territory between themselves, and the country's independence must be attributed to the Spanish-Portuguese struggle by Brazil and Argentina; had either been able to overwhelm the other, there would have been no Paraguay. Once independent, Paraguay attempted to settle its boundary disputes with Argentina and Brazil (1840-1862) to no avail. However, in 1865 Brazil intervened in Uruguay (which also owes its independence to unsettled Spanish/Argentine and Portuguese/Brazilian claims). This placed Paraguay in what seemed to be danger of Brazilian conquest and she attacked Brazil, but in order to do so crossed Argentine territory. Neither Brazil nor Argentina could allow the other to conquer Paraguay alone, so both, joined by Uruguay (q.v. below), declared war on Paraguay, and it seems all three were needed, for before Paraguay would give up, her population had been reduced from about 1,335,000 to less than 250,000; and of the survivors, only 28,746 were men (nine of every ten Paraguayan men were killed in that war). Argentina took the southern Chaco and what is now Misiones Povince, which incidentally sticks like a dagger into Brazil's underbelly, although the dagger was blunted in 1895 when Brazil chopped off part of what is now Brazil's Santa Catarina. Brazil also got all the land Paraguay had claimed north of the Apa River.

Its population replenished, Paraguay was ready for war with Bolivia (q.v. above) when Standard Oil began exploring for oil (1927) in the eastern Chaco. With loans from New York, an imported German general (von Kundt), and native Paraguayan machismo, Paraguay got most of the territory in dispute with Bolivia, but the 100,000 square miles that Paraguay gained cost a life a mile.

While Paraguay has retained independence since both Brazil and Argentina would rather it be independent than belong to the other, and neither is yet ready for war, it is estimated that over 80% of all Paraguayan industry is controlled by Brazilians or Argentines. An example of this is the mighty Casado ranch, owned by the Argentine family of that name. It is said to exceed five million acres in size and to account for 10% of all Paraguay's exports (cattle and quebracho). The only means of mechanized transport in the Paraguayan Chaco is the ranch's privately owned railroad, without which Paraguay could not have fought Bolivia.

Another Brazilian and Argentine reason for desiring to control Paraguay is the fact that Paraguay's rivers, which in large part are the borders with Brazil and Argentina, constitute the greatest untapped source of power in the world today, and both Argentina and Brazil desperately need power. A recent (1973) treaty with Brazil to build an eleven-million kilowatt hydro-electric facility (the largest in the world) seems to indicate that Brazil is besting Argentina in the struggle for control of Paraguay.

Uruguay. The Banda Oriental, or eastern bank (of the Uruguay River), as this country was called in colonial times, was, like Paraguay, the subject of armed struggle between Spain and Portugal. The latter founded a city (1679) right across the Plate estuary from the city of Our Lady of favoring winds (Buenos Aires); the eastern city, first called the colony of the Sacrament and today simply Colonia, was taken back and forth by the Spaniards and the Portuguese; the fomer eventually outflanked the Portuguese and built a fort and later a city at what is now Montevideo. When Buenos Aires became the capital of the Viceroyalty of La Plata, the Banda Oriental was incorporated into it and this was recognized by the Portuguese (Treaty of San Ildefonso, 1777). However, after the Argentines and Uruguayans had driven out the English, who made an abortive attempt to capture the Plate teritory in 1806/07, and secured their independence from Spain, the Portuguese again invaded Uruguay, capturing Montevideo and proclaiming the annexation of the Banda Oriental to Brazil (1821), calling it the Colonia Cisplatina (the prefix "cis" meaning "this side," in other words, "this side of Plate River"). Uruguayan patriots with Argentine help fought against the Brazilians, and eventually a treaty was signed (1828) in Montevideo under which both Argentina and Brazil recognized Uruguayan independence. Nevertheless, Argentina under the dictator Rosas did intervene in Uruguayan affairs in support of the Uruguayan leader Oribe, and the Blanco political party, and laid seige to Montevideo. In 1851 northern Uruguay went to Brazil. Rosas' fall from power (1852) did nothing to stop Uruguay's internal struggles. Perhaps sensing chaos and lack of active Argentine support, Brazil again invaded Uruguay in 1864 in support of the Colorado party against the Blanco party. Paraguay, interested in frustrating a Colorado victory which would have strengthened Brazil and raised a distinct threat to Paraguayan existence, intervened in favor of the Blancos, eventually sending troops across Argentina to attack southern Brazil (see "Paraguay" above). Since neither Brazil nor Argentina could allow the other to conquer Paraguay alone, they united to subdue Paraguay, allowing both Uruguay and Paraguay to retain their independence. As in the case of Bolivia, the existence of Paraguay and Uruguay seems to have been determined by the existence of strong neighbors.

Modern Uruguay is not unmindful of the existence of her powerful neighbors. The extreme left, the Tupamaros, are even said to feel that their depredations and especially any possibility of a leftist political victory in Uruguay, might very well bring on Brazilian intervention, since the Brazilian rightist dictatorship could not tolerate a center of insurgent activity so close to home. The Tupamaros presume that such intervention would rally all Uruguayans to their side (i.e., even rightist Uruguayans would support the left against a foreign invasion). History does not bear them out in this presumption, since Uruguayan parties have in the past accepted aid from Argentina and Brazil against other Uruguayans. But an Uruguayan Tupamaro leader has been quoted (1969) as saying that "there will be a fatherland for everyone, or there will not be a fatherland for anyone." This may have been a self-fulfilling prophecy, now (1973) that Uruguay is in pro-Brazilian rightist hands. Certain other factors make it seem that the possibility of Brazilian intervention is being closely watched by Argentina and other Spanish-speaking countries. When the Tupamaros were holding U.S. hostages and asking for the release of 150 political prisoners held by Uruguayan authorities, Brazil pressured Uruguay to make the deal but Argentina, backed by Venezuela, Colombia, Chile, and Peru supported the Uruguayan government's position not to deal (1970). Brazil, always aware that it is seen as a threat, cancelled military maneuvers scheduled to be held along the Uruguayan border just before the Uruguayan elections (1971/72) lest the maneuvers might give the impression that Brazil was prepared to intervene should the elections have resulted in a leftist victory, which they did not.

Despite its smallness, and despite today's political unheavals and economic crises, Uruguay is an agricultural treasure-trove; though its total area is small, virtually all of that area is usable for food production; Uruguayan cattle smuggled across the border into Brazil are gladly bought there at prices higher than can be obtained in price-controlled Uruguay itself.

Also, Uruguay is very important in the eventual control of the network of rivers draining into the Rio de la Plata. The Plate basin system of rivers reaches into northern Argentina, Bolivia, southern Brazil, Paraguay and, of course, Uruguay, and is of extreme importance to the economic development of all the countries involved, not only as a means of transportation but as a source of hydroelectric power.

E. THE INNER RIM

Soon after the discovery of what is known as America, but which was then thought to be the East Indies, Spain and Portugal disputed the ownership of the new lands. Acting as mediator, the Pope (1493) drew a line running due north-south through a point lying 100 leagues (300 miles) west of the Azores. Had this line been allowed to stand, Portugal would have had only a tiny toe-hold on the American mainland, since the agreement was that all land to the east of that line was Portuguese, and all land to the west was Spanish. However, Portugal complained that this line did not give her sufficient sea space to go eastward around Africa (a sailing vessel leaving Portugal must swing far to the west to avoid the calms of the Gulf of Guinea and come around the tip of Africa). Therefore, the line of demarcation was moved westward, and was now said to be a north-south line running through a point 370 leagues (1,110 miles) west of the Cape Verde Islands. Although it does not appear to have been known at that time, that line (which is about 45 degrees west longitude) runs through Brazil's eastern bulge, roughly from the mouth of the Amazon to Rio de Janeiro and gave Portugal a major beachhead on the South American continent. That is how Brazil was born, and in a manner of speaking, Brazil has been eating into the continent ever since (see Map B).

Although Brazil has remained until recent times a largely coastal civilization, its claims to the vast interior regions were, paradoxically, aided by the time of the so-called Portuguese "captivity" (1580-1640) during which Portugal was part of Spain. During this time Portuguese explorations into the interior went unstopped by the Spaniards, since all of South America was the common property of Spain, which included Portugal. When Portugal once again regained its independence from Spain, it was impossible or at least not thought worthwhile to reclaim the newly established Portuguese claims.

If one looks at a physical map of northern South America one sees a generally green area (lowlands) comprising the basins of the Orinoco and Amazon river systems. Most of this central but relatively unexplored and unmapped heartland is Brazilian; around the rim are nine countries or colonies (clockwise from the south: Paraguay, Bolivia, Peru, Ecuador, Colombia, Venezuela, Guyana, Surinam, French Guiana) only one of which (Ecuador) does not now have a common frontier with Brazil, although it once did (see below). We have spoken above about Brazilian relations with its southern neighbors Uruguay and Argentina, both of which also have common frontiers with Brazil (thus Brazil has common frontiers with all of South America's twelve other countries or colonies except two—Ecuador and Chile). Now we will examine the various disputes which exist along the rim of the jungle, some of which have concerned Brazil and a neighbor, and some of which have been between two or more of the rim countries.

The Treaty of San Ildefonso (1777, see Map B) between

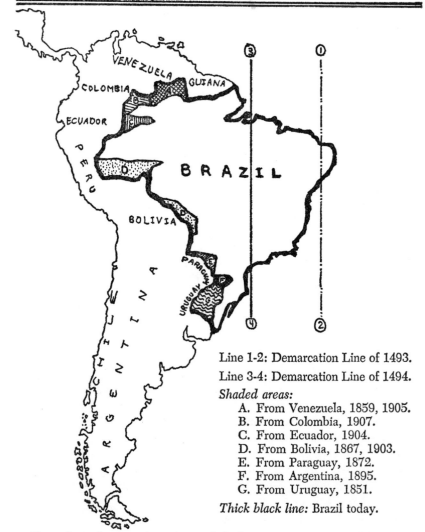

Line 1-2: Demarcation Line of 1493.

Line 3-4: Demarcation Line of 1494.

Shaded areas:
    A. From Venezuela, 1859, 1905.
    B. From Colombia, 1907.
    C. From Ecuador, 1904.
    D. From Bolivia, 1867, 1903.
    E. From Paraguay, 1872.
    F. From Argentina, 1895.
    G. From Uruguay, 1851.

Thick black line: Brazil today.

Note: Space between Line 3-4 and shaded areas largely acquired during 1580-1640 when Portugal was united with Spain.

Map drawn by Rosario Calabrese.

Spain and Portugal established part of what was to become Brazil; although it ceded Uruguay to Spain, it took a deep gouge into what was then the Spanish Viceroyalty of Peru, and this can be seen on the map today. This was based on prior claims but discovery of petroleum or other wealth or a general war between Brazil on the one side and Spanish-speaking South America on the other might reopen this issue. Certain large sections of territory that were deemed to have been Spanish by the Treaty have since been acquired by Brazil, including parts of what are now Argentina, Uruguay, Paraguay, Bolivia, Ecuador, Colombia and Venezuela (see Map B).

Ecuador. Like Bolivia, Ecuador has been sliced at by its neighbors over the years. Like Bolivia, it was tossed back and forth between two viceroyalties (that of Peru to the south and New Granada to the north). Up until 1717 it was part of the Peruvian viceroyalty, and was then removed from Peru and, together with what are now Venezuela and Colombia, was made part of the newly constituted viceroyalty of New Granada. When this new entity was abolished in 1723, Ecuador went back to Peru; when New Granada was reconstituted in 1740, Ecuador was again transferred. After Bolívar won New Granada's independence, he attempted to maintain the viceroyalty's integrity, calling the new country Gran Colombia. However, Venezuela and Ecuador withdrew from the federation (1829 and 1830 respectively), leaving three countries where there might have been one (see "The Accidental Countries" above for discussion of possible causes of the fragmentation of potentially strong viceroyalties into weak countries). Ecuador claims originally to have consisted of 400,000 square miles. Part of this claim is based on the fact that Ecuador is composed of what were two separate political divisions during colonial times, namely the *presidencia* of Quito and the *gobernación* of Guayaquil. What was then the presidency of Quito included 125,000 square miles of what is now, and has been since 1832, part of southern Colombia. The dismemberment of Ecuador continued in 1904, when 27,000 square miles of Amazonian territorry were yielded to Brazil (Tobar-Rio Branco Treaty), and in 1916, when 65,000 square miles of Amazonian territory were yielded to Colombia

(Muñoz Veruaza-Suárez Treaty). An additional 70,000 square miles went to Peru as a result of the Protocol of Rio de Janeiro of 1942, which settled the fighting between Peru and Ecuador in 1941 (although there was a flare-up in 1955). Of the original 400,000 square miles, Ecuador is now left with about 116,000 according to Ecuadorian figures, although there are still some remaining disputes. In 1971, the president of Ecuador (Velasco Ibarra) pointed out (somewhat tardily, it might seem) the need for strengthening Ecuador's armed forces to defend its frontiers. This may be quite significant in view of oil finds in Ecuadorian-Peruvian jungle regions near their present borders. This area has been in dispute before, and Ecuador has always claimed rights to the affluents to the Marañón River and then to the Amazon. Peru, surely not coincidentally, has employed the Grumman Ecosystems Corporation to map the jungle (1972). Texaco is also conducting oil explorations in Colombia, along Colombia's border with Ecuador (the Putumayo River), with an oil center to be built at Puerto Asís on that river. If, as appears possible, there is an underground lake of oil in Ecuadorian Amazonia between Colombia and Peru, and if the past history of chopping away at Ecuador is any indication, here is an obvious prize of war awaiting division by stronger neighbors. Brazil would appear to be out of the picture, unless it intervened to "save" Ecuador from Peru and Colombia, a possibility that will be considered in subsequent chapters.

A strong traditional interior division between two parts of Ecuador has also come down from colonial times, when, as mentioned earlier, there existed two political entities, Guayaquil and the surrounding lowlands, and Quito and the surrounding highlands. This division between *costeño* (coast dweller) and *serrano* (highlander) is still very much alive, and to what extent these two factions would resist separation is an open question. Also, there is the question as to what extent the Indians and possibly even the mestizos would resent or resist a change of flag if it meant (or they believed it to mean) improved economic conditions.

Peru-Colombia-Venezuela-Brazil-Guyana. The jungle area comprised of parts of these five countries is little known and poorly mapped. Ecuador was formerly involved but was cut out by territory yielded to Brazil, Colombia, and Peru (1904, 1916, and 1942 respectively, see "Ecuador" above). The boundaries between the Spanish and Portuguese territory were presumably settled in 1777 (Treaty of Ildefonso, see Map B), but Brazil since then has extended itself beyond the line drawn by that treaty and acquired land not only from Ecuador, but also Colombia (1907) and Venezuela (1859, 1905). Border disputes have also occurred between Peru and Colombia, starting as early as 1829; as late as 1932 Peru briefly occupied the so-called Leticia trapezium, a piece of land of roughly that shape between Brazil and Peru, intersected by the 70th west meridian about three or four degrees south of the equator. The northern boundary of this "trapezium" is the Putumayo River, along the banks of which oil has been found, so that it is a potential hot spot, although the Peruvian and Colombia state-owned oil companies signed a vaguely worded agreement in 1968 to "cooperate" on jungle oil. Trade between this region of Colombia and Peru is perhaps easier than with Bogotá. A future trouble spot to the east is Guyana (formerly British Guiana, now independent). Great parts of this country are claimed by Venezuela (everything west of the Essequibo River) and a smaller part by Surinam (Dutch Guiana). Should Great Britain and the Netherlands lose interest in Guyana and Surinam (which is not unlikely) and should Venezuela move to enforce her claims, one can only guess at Brazil's reaction (it is worth noting that Venezuela's claim alone is to well over half of Guyana). Venezuela's construction of a great new modern city at the confluence of the Orinoco and Caroni Rivers, first called Santo Tomé de Guayana and now Cuidad Guayana portends an intention to develop the Guayana highland, parts of which are in the now independent country of Guyana. These highlands comprise half of Venezuela without counting claims but contain only 3% of her population. The building of a dam on the Caroni also indicates Venezuela's intention to penetrate the area, which will be especially important if Venezuela's oil declines in value due to its high sulphur content; foreseeing this, Venezuela must diversify economically.

There do not appear to be major disputes between Colombia

and Venezuela in the jungle region, although there are some to the north, especially in the oil-rich Gulf of Venezuela. Some Venezuelan military and naval mobilization in and around LaGuajira peninsula was reported in 1971, and Colombia was adding units to her fleet in 1972 and 1973. More important perhaps as a source of friction between Venezuela and Colombia is the fact that 500,000 Colombians are said to be in Venezuela illegally (factory wages are four times as high in Venezuela). The presence of half a million illegal residents in a country with a total population of ten million is not a small matter, and the effect is sure to be heightened if recently discovered low-sulphur petroleum from other South American nations prices Venezuela's impure petroleum out of the market and brings a financial crisis to this till now oil-rich country.

Surinam. This self-governing overseas territory of the Netherlands has a population of 420,000 and does not appear to be of any particular value to the mother country. It is said that the major fear of the Surinamese is that the Netherlands might someday grant them independence. It is difficult to see, should that happen, how it could be kept out of the Brazilian orbit.

French Guiana. Unmentioned by us till now, this overseas department of France has a population of only 48,000, almost half of whom live in the capital city, and an area of 35,000 square miles. It is a drain on French economy. France's only apparent interest in keeping it (other than glory) is a rocket-launching pad built there by France, from which a few space probes have been launched. Should France lose interest in it, as in the case of Surinam, it should fall naturally into the Brazilian sphere of influence.

Panama. Panama had its own governor from 1514 to 1739, when it was incorporated into the viceroyalty of New Granada, and thus became part of Gran Colombia (composed of what are now Ecuador, Colombia and Venezuela). It tried to follow the example of Venezuela and Ecuador (which seceded from Gran Colombia in 1829 and 1830) by seceding itself in 1841, but was immediately recaptured by Colombia, again seceded in 1853 but returned voluntarily. A treaty between the U.S. and Colombia in 1846 (at which time Panama was part of Colombia) allowed the U.S. the right of transport across the Isthmus of Panama. In 1903, days after Colombia had refused to ratify a treaty with the U.S. regarding the building of a canal, Panama declared itself independent, and U.S. naval forces and Marines, invoking the 1846 treaty, prevented Colombia from attempting to again recapture Panama. Panama then signed a treaty with the U.S. allowing the Panama Canal to be built. If the Canal were to fall into disuse because of the construction of a better route through Nicaragua or northern Colombia or elsewhere, and if the U.S. were to lose interest in protecting Panama, it is conceivable that Colombia might again try to recapture it.

FOUR

Backwardness

La Croix, a French daily, said some years ago that Latin America is the greatest failure of Western civilization. Nevertheless, other observers, in what a South American might call *un derroche de eufonía,* a flooding-forth of euphemisms, have diligently scanned their dictionaries to come up with a list of presumably non-insulting words and phrases to describe the conditions of these nations. These include "underdeveloped," "recently emergent," "third world," "technologically non-advanced," "young nations," "client states" and so forth, but never "backward." But the terminology cannot mask the reality. The question remains: "Why are Latin American nations economically and military weak?" It is worthwhile to look at some of the explanations that have been offered.

The racial theory. This proposition holds that technological advance has been a function of whiteness; technology is a white European invention which has spread to the U.S. and the U.S.S.R. (both overwhelmingly white), and perhaps some other countries, and that within this white world it is the non-whites who are always the poorest (Chinese and Japanese might have to be excepted). This theory as held by white South Americans presumes the Negroids and Amerindians are naturally inferior, and it is the high concentration of these people that explains the economic backwardness of the South American nations. The theory fails to explain the constant economic crises of Argentina and Uruguay, both of which are overwhelmingly white; it is true, however, that the overall standard of living in those two countries is generally higher than in the heavily Amerindian countries such as Bolivia, Peru and Ecuador. However, even in the poorest countries, the white people have historically lived as well or perhaps better than whites in Europe or the U.S., and wealth tends to decrease in direct proportion to darkness of skin.

The ethnic theory. This theory sees technological advancement as native to northern Europe (England, Germany, Scandinavia) and holds that it declines as one moves southward through Europe, and that the southernmost countries of Europe are the poorest (Sicily, southern Spain, Portugal). Thus, when Europe exported its culture to the New World, it was only natural that the U.S. and Canada, populated, initially at least, mainly by nordics, would become technologically advanced, while South America, populated mainly by Andalusians, Portuguese, and Sicilians, would not.

The raw material theory. This concept holds that the flow of gold into Spain in the sixteenth century set up a syndrome that has existed to this day. According to this idea, England wanted to get its hands on the gold flowing into Spain, and therefore was motivated to, in effect, invent the industrial revolution in order to sell manufactured goods to Spain to get the gold. This, while on the one hand spurring on the technological development of England and that of its colonies, at the same time made it unnecessary for Spain to compete technologically since it could buy what was needed with the gold. This syndrome was passed on to Spain's colonies, which in their turn became suppliers of raw materials, with which they could buy essential manufactured goods without being obliged to develop their own industries; this led to economies based on the export of one or two raw materials, which made the South American nations dependent on low prices paid by the advanced nations for the raw materials, and victimized by the high prices charged for manufactured goods.

Head start. This theory holds that northern European countries simply got started first, but the economist David Felix points out that the vast majority of underdeveloped peoples and countries today were also underdeveloped two centuries ago by the technological standards of that age; the gap between the two has *merely widened* (emphasis added).[1] This of course merely moves the question of *why?* backwards in time. Felix probably feels that the essential difference is that advanced countries are innovators rather than borrowers, but even if that premise is granted, one may still ask *why* are some one and some the other?

The foreign villian and the evil oligarch. This theory places all blame on the foreigner, who, either as a Spaniard with a sword or a businessman with a checkbook, came, conquered and ever since has been systematically removing the country's wealth at profit to himself, all the while establishing puppet dictators to grind down the masses even more firmly into their abject poverty. By the non-white majorities, the oligarch is seen as allied with the foreign villian and in effect indistinguishable from him. The query that grows out of the "devil theory" is why have the majorities allowed this to happen to them, if indeed it is true that the foreign investor and the local oligarch are guilty as charged?

Fragmentation. Many observers blame the fragmentation of Spanish America into many small, weak countries rather than a few big, strong ones for the lack of development and economic strength. Sweden, with eight million people and an area of 175,000 square miles, is hardly huge when compared with Peru's more than thirteen million people and almost 500,000 square miles, yet the per capita income in Sweden is over $3,500 and in Peru $250, or about one-fourteenth. Nor is unfragmented Brazil small by any standards, and it still has a per capita income of only $350, or one-tenth of Sweden's. Another kind of fragmentation is also said to exist, in that liberal or leftist factions in the Hispanic world are constantly fighting each other, while traditionally rightist elements (the oligarchy, the Church, the military, the foreign investor) are generally unified. This, if once true, appears to be changing, and many cracks in the once monolithic right are appearing; for instance, socialist Allende was elected due to a split on the right.

[1]David Felix, "On Modernization, Economic Development and Humanization," talk prepared for 1969 Inter-American Forum held at Columbia University.

Recent emergence. The backwardness of certain nations is sometimes attributed to the fact that they are "only recently emerging," and while that might be the case elsewhere, that explanation can hardly serve in South America. Peru had a university in 1551 and a printing press in 1584; it is worthwhile remembering that the first English settlement in America was in 1607, and Harvard was founded in 1636.

Terrain and climate. Some observers give credence to the theory that the underdevelopment of South America is a result of deserts, jungles, mountains, poor communications, etc. Nevertheless the continent does contain vast accessible regions of high fertility; also, mineral wealth of every kind abounds and the potentialities for hydraulic power are almost limitless.

Overpopulation. This is a fashionable reason for underdevelopment, but South America has almost twice the area of the U.S. and only slightly greater total population.

Non-material values. This is today a distinctly unfashionable idea, at least among most young South Americans; it would hold that South America has opted to retain the old, true, traditional values of religion, family, and honor, and rejected the crass materialism of the north.

Internal disunity. It has also been adduced that most South American nations are not truly united; class struggle among the rich whites, the poorer mestizos or mulattos, and the very poor Indians and blacks prevent any kind of national unity or purpose; also, regionalism would be another debilitating factor, as between the *costeños* and *serranos* in Ecuador, or between the Argentines of the interior and the *porteños* (people of Buenos Aires).

The lack of a middle class. This is very popular with sociologists, who are quick to point out that all strong nations of modern times have a strong middle class; but the question then becomes, *why* is there only a small middle class in South America?

There may be more explanations for the economic weaknesses of the nations of South America, but the foregoing list catches most of the most commonly offered. There is, however, an additional reason we would like to bring forth for examination: despite all the squabbles and disputes and rival claims mentioned in the preceding chapter, "The Gifts of History," it is worthy of note that there have not been any real wars during the last ninety years (with the exception of the Chaco War and the Peruvian-Ecuadorian border fighting). Is it possible that technological advance and national unity and purpose only occur as a result of war or the threat of war, and that without technology and unity no nation can make the leap from backwardness to development?

FIVE

The Big One

By any standard, Brazil is not just one South American country: it is half the continent. All the other countries put together claim 3,617,734 square miles; Brazil alone claims 3,286,488. All of the rest of South America together has an estimated population of about 113,000,000; Brazil alone is over the 100,000,000 mark. Rather than speaking about "Latin" America, it might be wiser to refer to Spanish as opposed to Portuguese America. Indeed it has been suggested that the term Latin America was never dreamed of by the people within the area until it was revealed to them by journalists from the United States. However that may be, by sheer size alone, Brazil cannot be regarded as just one more Latin American country. But more than size differentiates Brazil from the other South American countries.

First of all, of course, is the fact that Brazil was colonized and settled by Portuguese rather than by Castilians; it is important in this context to underline the fact that the conquest and colonization of Spanish America was the work not of "Spaniards," if any such thing existed then (or now for that matter), but of Castilians. From the mid-thirteenth century on, the Iberian peninsula has been roughly divided into three regions, i.e., Portugal in the west, Castile in the center, and Aragon-Catalonia in the east. Although by the time of the discovery of America, Galicia, which linguistically belongs to Portugal, and the Basque country had been subsumed into Castile, and Castile was theoretically unified with Aragon-Catalonia under Ferdinand and Isabella and later under the Habsburg kings, the conquest and colonization of Spanish America was the work of Castilians, and to a lesser extent of Andalusians, who were included in the central kingdom of the peninsula. By royal decree, all trade had to be carried out by Castilians, and most officials sent by Spain

to America were Castilians, with little if any participation by
Galicians, Aragonese or Catalonians.

Although ethnic influences are difficult to pinpoint or express
statistically, no observer of the Spanish scene can deny that
historically there has been something different and unique about
the Castilians. They have seemed to place their trust in the
sword and the cross and the land, rather than in industry and
commerce. Industrial development in Spain took place in Catalonia (Barcelona) and the Basque country (Bilbao), and if
Madrid is now industrialized, it is also no longer a Castilian city.
The lineup was clear in the 1936-39 civil war, when Catalonia,
the Basques, and the proletariat of Madrid fought the soldiers,
farmers and priests of Castile and Andalusia in a vain attempt
to free themselves of Castilian rule, one of many such attempts.

As the gold from America flowed into Castile, it was used
to buy manufactured goods from England, rather than to develop industry in Spain, giving England (and the rest of Europe)
an industrial head start with which Spain was never to catch up.
The Spanish say, *"de tal palo tal astilla,"* or "a chip off the old
block"; true to their heritage, the colonies (later nations) of
Spain in America always depended on exporting raw materials
rather than developing their own industries. That Brazil may
become the first Iberoamerican nation to break this cycle may
be the result of its nonCastilian heritage.

Religiously, the Castilians have always manifested a ferver
rarely seen elsewhere in Christendom, with the possible exception of Ireland; under the Habsburg kings they expended enormous energy and treasure to stamp out any deviation from
dogma, both by profitless (to Spain) wars in Europe, and ruth-
less oppression at home (the Inquisition); without thought to
consequence they expelled their only bankers (the Jews) and
prohibited any Jew from going to the colonies. This is in sharp
contrast to the Portuguese, who did allow Protestants and Jews
to go to Brazil, and who never had the religious fervor (or per-
fervor) of the Castilians.

There was a period (from 1580 to 1640) when Spain and
Portugal *were* united under Spain (the Portuguese "captivity"),

and during this period the Inquisition *was* introduced into Brazil. Curiously enough, however, this "captivity," which ended in 1640 when Castile tried to use Portuguese troops to put down one of the many Catalonian rebellions, had beneficial effects insofar as Brazil is concerned, since the boundaries separating Spanish America from Portuguese America disappeared, facilitating great incursions of Brazilians into what was nominally Spanish territory (see Map B). These incursions were largely the work of *bandeiras* or prolonged family treks which lasted for years and penetrated as far as the silver mines of Peru and all the way to Bogota in Colombia. The people involved were mostly Paulistas (natives of São Paulo). Eventual formal recognition came with the Spanish-Portuguese Treaty of Ildefonso (1777, see Map B), but it is curious to note that the conquest of Portugal by Spain resulted in Portugal's colony Brazil more than doubling in size, at Spain's expense. There is no parallel development in the history of Spanish America.

Another fortuitous effect of the Portuguese "captivity" was the fact that it brought on attacks of Spain's enemies against the now-Spanish colony of Brazil, and from 1630 to 1654 Holland had a colony around Pernambuco, and it may very well be that the *concept* of Brazil was born during the fight to expel the Dutch, for it involved the people and resources of southern (particularly São Paulo) as well as northern Brazil, and was a Brazilian activity, since the mother country seemed content to let the Dutch remain. A purely colonial but sustained reaction to foreign invasion never occurred in Spanish South America, if one discounts a brief resistance by Buenos Aires against an abortive English attempt.

Another salient difference between the Spanish and Portuguese colonies in South America is that the latter were much earlier subjected to much more central control. At first Brazil was divided into hereditary captaincies-general (1533), each one with 50 leagues of coastline and extending indefinitely to the west, but as early as 1549 they were put under the control of a governor-general. This is in sharp contract to the viceroyalties of Spanish America, which not only did not unite among themselves but were in fact fragmented *within* themselves, with what were theoretically parts of a viceroyalty being actually independent entities in all but name. These subdivisions of the viceroyalties, variously called captaincies, *gobernaciones, presidencias,* etc., later became independent countries, in sharp contrast to what happened in Brazil.

The *manner* in which Brazil gained its independence also differs substantially from that of Spanish South America. The main factor of Spanish South American independence was the rivalry between the *criollo* and the *peninsular,* the former, the white native-born colonial, being deeply resentful of the privileges of the Spanish-born authorities sent to rule over him. When the Napoleonic invasions of the Iberian peninsula weakened Spain, the *criollos* of South America seized the opportunity to destroy what were in effect Spanish armies of occupation and gain their fragmented independence. The selfsame Napoleonic invasions caused the regent (later King John VI) of Portugal to flee to Brazil, where he was welcomed; Rio de Janeiro then became the capital of the Portuguese empire, a unique event in history. This period (1808-1822) gave Brazil a sense or "feel" of being a world power, and the equal of any European nation, which it retains to this day. The defeat of Napoleon and the shortsightedness of a Cortes (parliament) meeting in Lisbon for the first time in 100 years forced John to return to Portugal, leaving his son Dom Pedro as regent in Brazil. A majority of the Cortes wanted to restore Brazil to its former colonial status, which was unacceptable to the *mazombos* or *criollos* of Brazil, and the regent Dom Pedro was declared Emperor of Brazil under a constitutional monarchy. Although forced to abdicate in 1831 in favor of his five-year-old son and despite a chaotic regency that lasted until 1840, when the son assumed the throne as Pedro II, the period of the Brazilian Empire (1822-1889) provided Brazil with a long period of legitimate government during her first decades of life as an independent nation, such as was not enjoyed by any of the Spanish-speaking nations of South America. It also kept Brazil unified and prospering.

The eventual fall of the monarchy, and its replacement by

a quasi-republican form of government, is at first sight difficult to understand, since the reign of Pedro II had brought tremendous progress to Brazil. Among many explanations, one may cite the fact that both the right and the left had turned against him. The slave-owners were hostile to him because he had freed the slaves. His actions against certain bishops deprived him of the support of the Church, which, if not as powerful as in Spanish America, did (and does) wield considerable influence. Also, his attempts to keep the armed forces out of politics lessened his support by the military. Also, the growth of "republicanism" as an acceptable political doctrine was a major factor in reducing his support from the left. Even so, all these factors might have been overcome had it not been for his illness and the personal unpopularity of his daughter Isabel, heiress-apparent to the throne. Nevertheless, the tremendous growth during the Empire made Brazil the major power of the continent, and gave Brazil a sense of unity that has endured. An interesting commentary on Brazilian monarchy vis-à-vis Spanish American republicanism was spoken in 1889, when the president of Venezuela, told of Pedro's abdication, said that the Empire of Brazil had been the only true republic of South America. Brazil's experience with constitutional monarchy lends credence to the thesis of those Latin Americanists who feel that Spanish America ought to have opted for this form of government rather than the sham republicanism in Spanish South America. In any event, the *manner* of Brazil's independence, and the resulting constitutional monarchy, clearly differentiate it from Spanish South America.

The period between the fall of the Empire and the definitive military takeover (1889-1964) is a time during which, superficially at least, Brazil seems to have acted more like other South American countries, organized as a sham republic with the armed forces always in the wings as "guarantors" of constitutional process, with a surfeit of coups d'état, palace revolutions, corruption, etc. Roughly the first half of this period, the so-called "old republic," was ended by the "new state" proclaimed by Getulio Vargas after his take-over of power in 1930. It is interesting to note that he was aided by a group of young military officers, the *tenentes*; this is a tendency we will refer to again later. Although sometimes cruel and always totalitarian, Vargas moved toward improved conditions for the working man, and toward diversification of the economy and a lessening of the absolute dependence on agriculture, coffee in particular (Brazil throughout its history had up until then been, at one time or another, overly dependent on a single crop, at first brazilwood, then sugar, then gold, then wild rubber and finally coffee).

One aspect of Vargas' first period of rule was that, during it, Brazil actually participated in World War II, in sharp differentiation with other South American countries, whose participation was generally limited to declaring war once it was definite that Germany was going to lose. Brazil on the other hand took active part in the naval and land war, sending troops to fight in Italy. This was wryly criticized by Brazilians, who only half mockingly said that the generals and admirals were devoting too much time to their hobby, war, rather than their real business of running the country. Those generals and admirals may soon find a way to combine their hobby with their real business, if this writer's theory is correct. In any event, Vargas was overthrown in 1945 and followed by the civilian election of a general and a move toward increased political democracy, but with the armed forces as always constitutionally named as guarantors of constitutional powers. Vargas was permitted to reassume the presidency in 1951 by the same armed forces that had ousted him in 1945, but his popular base of support had disintegrated, and when asked to resign by the armed forces in 1954 he killed himself. It was during Vargas' second term in office that *"o petróleo é nosso"* (the oil is ours) became the nation's rallying cry, and the state oil company Petrobrás was formed. This essentially socialistic doctrine of state ownership of the nation's oil resources became so deeply ingrained in the national consciousness that none dared oppose it, not even the most conservative.

After some infighting and coups and counter-coups, Kubitschek and Goulart took office as president and vice-president in 1956. They promised 50 years' progress in five, and their election was a clear vindication of Vargas, since they were his political heirs. The ever-present but muted conviction that Brazil was destined to become a world power was now loudly proclaimed, and the government entered the fields of highway construction, hydroelectric power, and fossil-fuel, iron and steel production to an unprecedented degree. The new capital Brasília, deliberately conceived and designed to turn the eyes of coastal Brazilians westward and inward to the heart of the continent and the last great frontier, was built. But all this was not without a price, as the foreign debt doubled and the cost of living tripled and corruption became so bad as to disgust even Brazilians, who know something about it. It was probably this latter factor that resulted in the defeat of Kubitschek's candidate in the 1960 elections, and the election instead of Jânio Quadras, a political maverick whose campaign symbol was a new broom. By a quirk of fate, however, Goulart (Kubitschek's man) was again elected vice-president. Quadras' election was the first substantial defeat of the Vargas forces in thirty years, but it was to be short-lived. With no control of congress, he felt unable to govern and resigned after only seven months in office, at a time when the vice-president Goulart was in Singapore after a state visit to Communist China. The armed forces split as to whether or not to allow Goulart to assume the presidency; this split brought the country to the verge of civil war between the two military factions. A compromise solution installed Goulart as a figurehead president, but the powers of the presidency were later restored to him after a plebiscite. Nonetheless, the cost of living tripled in his two years in office, and the gross national product stopped growing, after years of regular growth, despite (or because of) Goulart's attempts to implement socialistic measures. The military would, however, probably have allowed him to complete his lawful term of office had it not been for his tactic of attempting to undermine the power of military officers by building a personal following among enlisted men. This reached intolerable (to the officers) limits when Goulart supported a strike by naval enlisted personnel, and the armed forces took power and

Goulart fled to exile (April 2, 1964). With this date begins what this writer would call *a época do porvir,* the time of the future, in Brazil certainly and perhaps in all of South America.

A keen if not widely known student of Brazilian affairs, Frank D. McCann, said in 1969 that the Brazilian military were searching for a formula to replace the Empire, i.e., to create a point of convergence of the national aspirations. Just what form this concept might take cannot yet be clearly foretold, but one can by no means ignore the tremendous importance of the Escola Superior de Guerra (ESG), a conscious attempt to create a ruling intellectual elite. As McCann correctly pointed out in 1969, this institution is by no means a retreat of the military to the barracks, nor a simple place of instruction in battlefield tactics. More designed to militarize civilians than to train the military, it seems a deliberate attempt to create a corps of dedicated officers and civilians who will be able to enunciate and implement the national ideal and purpose. It has been suggested that many of the purges in Brazil's universities have not been aimed so much at getting rid of dissidents but rather of making room for ESG graduates in the vacated professorships. The president-designate of Brazil for the 1974-79 term, Ernesto Geisel, is one of the founders of ESG.

While the ESG is not for the purpose of teaching battlefield tactics, it would be a mistake to forget it is a *war* school, but the war involves the total problem of moving Brazil into the ranks of the industrialized world powers. This may eventually involve actual fighting, but it also involves the development of industry, the shipping of goods to and from Brazil in Brazilian bottoms rather than in foreign ships, the opening up of the vast interior of the country, the securing of fuel and power, the registering of antarctic claims, the viewing of world affairs from a strictly Brazilian viewpoint, as opposed to the acceptance of foreign propaganda (such as the simplistic U.S. concept of a world divided between Communist and "free" nations). It is probable that the ESG sees U.S. power declining and being replaced by four or five power centers, one the U.S. itself, another the European Economic Community, another the U.S.S.R. and its European satellites, still another Japan, and eventually (if not already) China. Presumably, one major policy will be to avoid South America slipping out of the failing grasp of the U.S. only to drift into another (non-Brazilian) sphere of influence, or, if the concept of spheres of influence dies out among the advanced nations, to remain a simple source of raw materials. To achieve all this, many things are necessary; some are evident and some can be guessed.

First and foremost, Brazil will want to continue the sensational growth of its exports and gross national product, but without unduly increasing labor costs. João Paulo dos Reis Velloso, Minister of Planning, writing in the New York *Times* in January 1973, proudly says that in 1964 Brazil's GNP was stagnant at $26.5 billion, but that it is now (only nine years later) approach-$53 billion; this rate of growth outruns inflation and outpaces the rest of the continent; he goes on to point out that exports in 1963 were $1.4 billion, and in 1973 should go over $4.5, which is to say that the GNP has doubled and exports tripled in less than ten years. It is particularly important to note that an ever greater percentage of the exports consist of manufactured goods, including computers, heavy road-building and electrical equipment, ships and motor vehicles. The rate of inflation has, during the same period, declined from 100% a year to 16% in 1972 and a probable 12% in 1973. In essence, the above is the Brazilian economic miracle.

But to continue the miracle-working, wages in Brazil must be kept down, both to make exports of manufactured goods competitive, as well as to prevent the Brazilian workers from overconsuming goods that ought to be exported. For instance, starting in 1974 Ford plans to buy 200,000 engines from Brazil instead of building them in Detroit; clearly, Ford does this because of the lower labor costs in Brazil. If those costs go up appreciably, Ford will give those jobs back to American workers.

Some observers may feel that the wage differential is so great that this is not a real problem, but even before Brazilian wages begin to equal American wages, they will be getting as high as Japanese or Taiwanese wages, and Ford would just as soon buy from one place as another. So somehow Brazil must keep its workers happy at lower wages. For the moment this is possible since so many people have been so poor for so long, but desire grows exponentially. Today's Brazilian, however poor his parents might have been, sees television and the movies; he sees the shops filled with the good things, and he will surely want them. As he becomes more and more educated (and the government is spending enormous sums to educate him) he will realize that he is working for $100 a month to make television sets for American workers who are earning ten times that much. Will he be content? (The falling value of the dollar is an unpredictable factor in future U.S.-Brazilian trade.)

Brazil will also resist foreigners who warn of the dangers of overpopulation, of pollution, of damage to the ecology. Considering that Brazil is as big as the continental U.S. and has less than half as many people, Brazilians take a dim view of Americans warning them of overpopulation; also, the more people there are, the more they have to compete for jobs, which tends to keep wages down. Brazilians (and for that matter Latin Americans in general) resent Americans and Europeans warning them not to pollute; they feel that it is the advanced nations that have created most of the pollution in the world today, and that those advanced nations ought to clean up at home themselves first before advising others. Industrialization in Latin America is difficult enough, they say, without the added costs of antipollution, which would drive up prices of manufactured goods. Brazil in particular needs to develop its hinterland, the great Amazon rain forest; warnings of worldwide catastrophe if this is done too quickly or badly are apt to fall on unhearing Brazilian ears, although there is some indication that the dangers inherent *to Brazil* of slash-and-burn farming in the jungle are being thought about (hopefully in the ESG).

Limited proven deposits of fossil fuels, particularly of oil, pose a problem of major proportions. At the present time Brazil produces only about a third as much oil as it needs, and the need is constantly growing. This problem is being attacked in two ways: (1) domestic exploration, including offshore drilling as far as 85 miles out to sea, and (2) negotiations with foreign countries for joint ventures; among the nations involved are Bolivia, Ecuador, Iraq, Peru, Venezuela and others including several in the Near East. One result of Brazil's dependence on oil that has to be transported in ships will undoubtedly be a strong navy, and a ten-year plan was started in 1967 aimed at raising the number of units in the Brazilian navy from 65 to 137, aiming at eventual control of the South Atlantic. The creation (1973) of a Brazilian submarine fleet is indicative of this policy. Part of this strategy would involve friendly relations with African nations with South Atlantic coastlines and a possible attempt to involve Brazil in a pan-African movement, trading on the many people of Negro background in Brazil. What Africa has to sell Brazil except oil is a question, however.

A more immediate possibility, however, would be control of proven oil reserves in the jungles of Bolivia, Ecuador, and Peru. These reserves, some only recently found, are on or near Brazil's frontiers. The oil is now (or will soon be)piped over the Andes to the Pacific, and then by sea to the U.S. This is a wrong-way flow from the Brazilian viewpoint, and it is not beyond imagination that some old frontiers may change. A recent (1973) presidential decree in Brazil provided for the formation of five battalions of infantry specially trained for jungle warfare, to be stationed in the jungle.

The immense hydroelectric potential of the rivers of southern Brazil, most of which border neighboring countries, may be seen as another possible prize of war or economic control by Brazil of her neighbors. The development of battery-driven vehicular transportation and electrified railroads in order to use hydroelectric energy as a substitute for oil is a possibility, and might move Brazil toward becoming an innovative nation technologically, rather than a borrower. Another possible substitute power source is atomic power, and Brazil certainly has both the technology and the uranium and has incidentally refused to sign the nonproliferation of atomic arms treaty, which was seen in Brazil as a rigged attempt by the U.S. and the U.S.S.R. to keep the poor nations both weak and poor.

In addition to beefing up it forces in the South Atlantic and in the jungle, Brazil is also preparing for air war, and has recently obtained a $60 million air traffic control facility which can also function as an air-defense radar system. Perhaps more significantly, it is said that by the end of the seventies, Brazil will be building aircraft similar to the French Mirage, some of which it has already bought from France. (An interesting sidenote on Brazilian aviation is that many Brazilians feel that the first heavier-than-air flights were made *not* by the Wright brothers, but by the Brazilian Alberto Santos-Dumont, in France in October and November of 1906. The Wright brothers claimed to have flown such an aircraft in 1903, but there were apparently no disinterested witnesses to that event. The first *public* flight by the Wrights was in 1908. The important thing about this controversy is not who is right, but that Brazilians feel that they are innovative and not purely a borrowing culture.)

A perennial problem of Brazil, discussed partially above, is the matter of the development of the rain forest into something useful. This will not be easy, as can be seen by this description of the ecology of the Amazonian rain forest given by Alan Anderson: "Under natural forest conditions, few demands are made of the soil. It is protected from the sun by the deep shade of the jungle canopy, and from the beating rain by a constantly renewed carpet of decaying leaves, branches and tree trunks. Under these near-constant conditions, the litter is decomposed quickly by over 500 kinds of micro-organisms into inorganic nutrients which are just as quickly captured by the dense, shallow-root network of tropical trees. The efficiency of this system is very high. There is practically no soil erosion or escape of nutrients. Even the heaviest rains are slowed by the mulch, so that plant roots have time to absorb it. Wilhelm Brinkham, a German ecologist now working at the new Amazon Research Institute near Manaus, describes this system as self-contained. 'The rain brings no nutrients of importance. The river carries away none. Since they are not found in the soil either, the forest lives on itself.' When the forest is removed, the system breaks down. There is no more leaf and branch litter to cover the ground. Rain leaches easily through the porous soil, carrying soluble nutrients deep beyond the reach of plant roots. Under forest conditions, one hectacre (2.5 acres) of soil loses only two pounds of soil a year to erosion; when the trees are cut, the same area loses 34 *tons* of soil a year. Such exposed soil may readily be laterized, or turned to stone."[2]

Since the Brazilian government is looking toward the rain forest as potential farming land, and is sending thousands (and eventually hundreds of thousands) of people from the impoverished and drought-ridden northeast into the jungle as homesteaders to clear the land and plant crops, it may be that the world's biggest parking lot is in the process of being created, if the exposed soil does in fact turn to stone. No one can say for certain what the outcome will be if present plans continue. It is said that today there are 30,000 men doing nothing but cutting down the forest, and past experience has shown that cleared land in the rain forest is good for one, two or three harvests only. Alternative plans include conversion of the forest into pasture, but this would entail heavy fertilization of the pastures, which would tend to make the meat too expensive. Some experts lean toward the idea of perpetuating the forest, but substituting other trees such as rubber, cacao, babaçu, etc., or using existing trees for lumber and paper (of which there may soon be a worldwide shortage) but replenishing them so that the forest continues to live. In the previously cited article, Anderson points out that "the only successful farmers in the Amazon so far have been a handful of immigrant Japanese . . . (who) are masters of organic techniques, and by conscientious manuring and mulching they have been able to avoid the yield drop-off typical of Brazilian slash-and-burn farming." Whatever the eventual solution, if there is to be any, the utilization of this vast area must be a matter of prime concern for the leaders of Brazil.

A social problem of great potential magnitude is the matter of race; Brazilians are prone to say that no race problems exists in Brazil, but certain as yet inconclusive trends strongly suggest that the new jobs being created by Brazil's growing industries

[2]Alan Anderson, "Devastation on the Amazon?" *Organic Gardening and Farming,* November, 1972, p. 90 et seq.

are going to whites and *pardos* (mulattos) and not to the blacks. This may tend to create a subclass of poor blacks making up about 11% of the population as opposed to 88% whites and *pardos* (with at present about one percent of Orientals). Brazilians speak of a process of *branqueamento,* or whitening, as intermating has produced more and more *pardos,* who tend to be regarded as whites rather than blacks (the direct opposite of the United States). However, if economic segregation and social ostracism are applied to the true blacks, this process may be halted, and a static group of poverty and discontent created.

Returning for a moment to the Escola Superior de Guerra, it is said that many of the younger graduates are somewhat resentful of the aging flag officers who at present control Brazil's armed forces; it seems to this observer, however, that it is unlikely that the younger men will do anything to upset the existing order, since strife within the armed forces might ruin the entire structure. It seems more likely that the younger men will await the inevitable toll of time, and gradually themselves (the new "tenentes") assume control of the armed services, and of the nation. This will place a consciously prepared and carefully nurtured intellectual elite in charge of one of the fastest-growing nations of the world. Whether they will be content to follow the "borrower" psychology that dominates Brazil (as witness the dependence on foreign capital and foreign technological know-how) or whether they will look for new and innately Brazilian solutions, is yet to be seen.

The incoming president of Brazil, scheduled to serve from 1974 to 1979, is the son of German immigrants, and thus unconnected to the old oligarchy, and is not by heritage either Portuguese or African; yet he is certainly 100% Brazilian; a polygot and a chessplayer and a founder of the Escola Superior de Guerra, he just may be ideally suited to really understand Brazil since as an immigrant's son he can see it whole, and yet not bear the stigma of belonging to any one of the traditional classes and thus not be the object of any prejudice (as he might be if he were black or brown or Portuguese-white or an immigrant himself).

SIX

Difficulties of Creating a Spanish-Speaking Bloc

The last gasp of U.S. imperialism in South America may be the Latin American Free Trade Association (LAFTA, known in Spanish as ALALC for Asociación Latinoamericana de Libre Comercio), an almost frivolous plan touted by Lyndon Johnson, perhaps as an attempt to salvage something from the dregs of Kennedy's bankrupt Alliance for Progress. Doomed from conception, LAFTA would have divided industrial hegemony in Latin America between Buenos Aires and São Paolo, and was thus entirely unacceptable to either of the two main contenders for control of South America, Argentina and Brazil; had the plan by some miracle been effectively implemented, it would have reduced the other South American nations to economic peonage, and so was unacceptable to them. The thought behind this almost unbelievable U.S. proposal was presumably to give U.S. industry and multinational corporations a chance to control, by capital exportation to, and exploitation of the rivalry between, the Buenos Aires and São Paolo megalopolises, a new source of low-cost labor and a monopoly of the Latin American "common" market. That there existed any real hope in Washington that South America would tolerate this is scarcely credible; surely its inevitable failure must have been pointed out to the then (1967) Secretary of State, Rusk; that he persevered is indicative only of his invincible ignorance of things South American.

We dredge up the specter of the moribund LAFTA only to point out the sharp contrast between it and today's Andean Pact, an attempt of six Spanish-speaking nations of South America to form something more than a common market; while it is true that all the members are situated in the Andean region (Chile, Bolivia, Peru, Ecuador, Colombia, Venezuela), it is also important to note that these six nations together have almost three times as many people as Argentina and double the area. Joseph Novitski, a former *New York Times*man and one of the keenest observers of the Latin American scene writing today (although no longer for the *Times*) correctly pointed out in August 1972 that, "If Argentina were to join the Andean Group, it would effectively divide South America into two trading and development blocs—Brazil on the one side and the rest on the other. But that, Andean group officials say, is not their intention." Intentional or not, it is hardly to be denied that the Brazilian economic miracle has hastened and strengthened the growth of the Andean Group by providing an incentive. The addition of Argentina with its comparatively great industrial capacity would certainly strengthen the Group, but the prospect cannot be entirely pleasurable to the present members, precisely because of Argentina's economic strength. After all, Argentina's 1971 GNP of almost $32 billion was not far behind the $34 billion total of the other six combined, despite their far greater population and area. Together this is a total of $66 billion, as opposed to Brazil's US$40 billion GNP that same year. The Spanish-speaking worry is that Brazil's GNP is increasing at a far greater rate than theirs; 1975 figures will be very interesting to look at. But before the dangers presented by Brazil are faced, the present six members of the Andean Group will have to take a long hard look at the possible consequences of taking the Argentine fox into the Andean henhouse.

Unmentioned by Novitski are two other Spanish-speaking South American countries (Paraguay and Uruguay) which do not seem to be even being considered for membership in the Andean Group. Either one of these countries is a potential casus belli between Argentina and Brazil, and thus inclusion of Argentina into the Andean group would (if the Group became in fact a military alliance) bring in its train the possibility that the six Andean nations would be sucked into an Argentine-Brazilian war when they might prefer to let Argentina and Brazil fight it out in the hopes that they might weaken each other. On the other hand, they might risk this in order to create a solid Spanish-speaking bloc to contain possible Brazilian expansion.

One reason for this is that the six-member Andean group as presently constituted includes Bolivia, a weak spot from any standpoint, and a natural target for Brazilian economic and/or military penetration.

As an alternative to Argentina, or at least as a counterbalance, the Andean Group is attempting to enter into close relationship with faraway but Spanish-speaking and economically powerful Mexico (a 1971 GNP equal to Argentina's US$32 billion). An example of this was the signing (December 1972) of two pacts between Mexico and the Andean Group, the first providing a $5 million line of credit to the Group, and the second a million-dollar loan to study possible common interests of the Andean Development Corporation (in Spanish CAF for Corporación Andina de Fomento) and Mexico. While neither pact is in itself earthshaking, the idea of Mexican-Andean cooperation may be a significant trend.

The Andean Group is, as Novitski points out, more than a customs union or a common market. Specific industries have been assigned to each of the member countries, who are committed to exact ways of sharing plants that will supply the whole market with the particular product within a stipulated time. No one member can compete with another in the manufacturing of the particular products, unless competition is agreed upon. All members must buy them from one another without tariffs and without importing the specified products from outside the Group. Naturally, there are many products that are not made within the Group; while some of these needs can be filled by newly created industries, a certain amount of importation will continue to be necessary. It is obvious that the addition of Argentina would significantly affect the existing plans. Motor vehicle production, a sine qua non for developing economies, is an important example of what is lacking.

In 1970, Brazil produced 415,000 motor vehicles, Argentina 220,000 and the rest of South America negligible quantities (Mexico produced 186,000). Either Mexico or Argentina (or both) could supply motor vehicles; what is not so clear is what the six-member Andean Group could supply in return, since the

traditional export products of the six flow naturally to the U.S., Europe or Japan (Bolivia, tin; Chile, copper; Peru, minerals, fishmeal, sugar, etc.; Colombia, coffee; Ecuador, fruit and oil; Venezuela, oil), and it is unlikely that these traditional export products will be required in substantial amounts in either Mexico or Argentina in the foreseeable future. Without Argentina and Mexico a likely solution is a factory built within the Group, but this raises the question whether the Group without Argentina can attract foreign capital, or exist without it. The reference here is not to capital destined to exploit raw materials (oil or mining companies, for instance). In these cases, the product is destined for sale outside of the Group's area. This type of investment will probably not be affected by the existence of the Group per se. We are speaking rather about the investment of capital to produce products to be sold within the Group, as for instance a Volkswagen plant to produce vehicles to be sold within the Group.

It is doubtful that, at this time, there exists sufficient available risk capital, either in the private or public sector, to finance the creation of an Andean Group automobile industry. If the necessary capital has to be imported, it will necessarily have to come from the U.S. or Europe or Japan, and it will be private capital, which means that the investment can only be made if the company (be it Ford or Volkswagen or Toyota) deems that there is either (1) a sufficient market within the Group to justify the investment, or (2) that the Group will allow a percentage of the vehicles made to be exported. The first possibility is doubtful on a short-term basis, although a company might be tempted if promised a long-term monopoly of 20 or 30 years, by which time the market should have grown sufficiently to make the franchise worthwhile and justify the original investment. A stumbling block is the insistence of 51% control of the company by the Group itself; this insistence, if continued, might dampen the inward flow of capital. The second alternative of allowing the foreign company to take advantage of the cheap labor available within the Group to manufacture for export, as Brazil does, is a possibility, but, as in the case of Brazil, depends on

keeping labor costs down, and to a certain extent defeats the purpose of the Group itself. Nevertheless, this solution may be unavoidable. Still another difficulty in attracting this kind of foreign capital is the fact that some of the member nations are socialist or tending that way, while others are capitalist.

In any event, the division of South America into two blocs, one Spanish-speaking and the other Portugese, is not simple. The Portuguese-speaking part, for one thing, will be continuously trying to divide the Spanish-speaking part, and infiltrate it with loans, etc. Such overtures (and actual loans) have already been made by Brazil to Uruguay, Paraguay, Bolivia, Peru, Ecuador, Colombia, Venezuela and Guyana in South America alone, as well as to the countries of Central America (this incursion into Mexico's "sphere of influence" may be a counterbalance to Mexico's flirtation with the Andean Group). The actual amounts involved are small if compared to past U.S. aid, but as other sources of aid dry up, Brazil's may seem larger and larger.

A particularly significant development was the signing by Brazil of a partnership agreement with Paraguay to build what is expected to be the world's largest hydrolectric power facility. To be located at Itaipú on the Paraná River, which is the border between Brazil and Paraguay, it is expected to have a capacity of eleven million kilowatts. The power is to be divided equally between the two countries, but Paraguay would immediately sell a good part of its half back to Brazil, since the smaller country would have no use for that much power. Financing of the $2 billion project has reportedly been offered by the U.S., the U.S.S.R. and Japan. Brazil's growing power needs being what they are, the project should have no difficulty in paying for itself. It is scheduled for completion in 1992. The signing of this accord was a sharp blow to Argentina on three counts. First, the planned Brazilian-Paraguayan dam might wreck the possibility of two hydrolectric installations that Argentina wanted to build with Paraguay further down the same river; second, the lowering of the river's water level due to the dam might destroy its usefulness as a navigable stream and possibly ruin the Argentine

river port of Rosario. Perhaps most importantly from the
Argentine standpoint, the new dam would guarantee that
Brazilian industry would have enough power to continue its
growth during the foreseeable future, and become stronger vis-
à-vis Argentina. Ex-dictator Juan Perón of Argentina attempted
to intervene with his personal friend Stroessner, dictator of
Paraguay, to postpone the signing, but to no avail. Not only
that, but the Paraguayan foreign minister shortly afterward
stated that Paraguay would not enter into any accord with
another country without prior approval by Brazil. If this is
indeed to be Paraguay's position, it would be a clear indication
that Paraguay is moving into Brazil's sphere of influence, a major
crack in the by no means monolithic "alliance" of Spanish-speaking South America.

Brazil is, as we have seen before, also interested in eastern
Bolivia, especially the oil to be found there; this region of
Bolivia has already tried to secede and join Brazil, and may
again. Major portions of the jungle regions of Bolivia near the
border are populated by Brazilians. Brazil has also provided
economic aid to Bolivia, and there were rumors late in 1972 that
Brazil might offer Bolivia some sort of egress to the Atlantic via
inland waterways.

Brazil's interest in her southern "accidental" neighbors does
not of course exclude Uruguay, and since that country's main
products (meat and cereals) are competitive with Argentina's,
it is quite likely that Uruguay is a far more logical trading part-
ner of Brazil than of Argentina.

In general, Brazil could, without too much difficulty, find
other ancient rivalries among the Spanish-speaking nations of the
continent to exploit (see Chapter Three, "The Gifts of History"),
so that formation of an anti-Brazilian bloc is not going to be
easy.

But perhaps the most important factors opposing the unity of
Spanish-speaking South America are not international, but internal to the several countries themselves. A prime example of
this is Brazil's main rival for leadership, Argentina, which faces
three continuing crises: first of all, despite the overwhelming

victory of the Peronists in the 1973 elections, Argentines of all political leanings must face up to the fact that the man Juan Domingo Perón is certain, sooner or later, to die (even any public evidence of senility would be enough); what will happen to the so-called Peronist coalition in that event cannot of course be foretold with certainty, but present indications are that it would fragment, the Peronists would be unable to govern, and the military would be forced to attempt to retake control, probably bringing on civil war. The constant knowledge that the country is one heartbeat away from chaos can hardly aid Argentina in its efforts to lead Spanish-speaking South America.

Another factor inhibiting Argentina's internal stability is the meat-eating propensity of the Argentines. Beef consumption in Argentina is the highest of any nation in the world, but this gluttony has had dire consequences. During his first term in power Perón forced the farmers to sell agricultural products in general at ruinously low prices, in order to provide cheap beef to the *descamisados* (as he called his impoverished supporters), or to resell abroad and thus generate funds to be used for industrialization. The result was the ruination of the great Argentine herd. At the beginning of this century there were over five animals per person, which dropped to less than two. Although the ratio is increasing and is now over two per person, the regrowth has been accomplished by meatless weeks, and it was perhaps this more than anything else that contributed to the Peronist victory. Now that they are in power, the Peronists will either be forced to continue the meatless policy, and thus earn the disfavor of the mass of the people, or resume providing cheap beef at subsidized prices, which will both drain the treasury and decrease exports (if Argentina is to have any hope of exporting over the $3 billion mark in 1973, it will have to sell at least US$1 billion of meat and meat products abroad, which it cannot do if it is to supply cheap beef to the populace). The need to export is critical, since coal, iron ore and above all oil must be imported just to keep the industrial plant running at its present levels; exports have to be increased if capital expansion is contemplated. If the industrial plant is not kept running

and growing, of course, it will produce less, exports will fall, unemployment will soar, and chaos will prevail. But if the Peronist government refuses to provide cheap beef (and admittedly the term is being used simplistically to cover a whole range of government concessions to the working classes), there is some question that it will be able to continue to govern.

Thus Argentina today lives in constant fear of a political crisis if Perón dies, which he inevitably must, and of an economic crisis if cheap meat is provided at the expense of exports, and of a political crisis if it is not.

Sawing away at the slender thread preventing this double-edged Damoclean sword from destroying Argentina is a third factor: terrorism from the extreme left, involving kidnapping, robbery, murder, riots, demonstrations, etc. If this is allowed to continue unchecked, the country will revert to chaos; if it is halted by strong military action, the result might be to deprive the Peronist coalition of the support of its left wing.

Another example of internal stresses within the Spanish-speaking countries is the expectations of the middle class. Over the years, many Latin Americanists have been prone to say that one of the main reasons for Latin American underdevelopment has been the lack of a middle class. Paradoxically, in certain countries today (notably Argentina, Uruguay and Chile, but also in lesser degree in others) it is the middle class whose demands and pressures are serving to weaken existing governments. The three countries mentioned have always had the largest middle classes in South America; these people are literate and aware of world conditions. They are largely white and have no background of having been told that they are inferior or must expect less because they are blacks or Indians. They know about the mechanical devices possessed by their counterparts in the U.S. and Europe (automobiles, refrigerators, washers, dryers, toasters, the list is endless) and they want them. However, they also know about the life of leisure and the servants of the upper classes in their own countries, and they want those also, and they can't have both, but they want both. The Peronists of Argentina (or for that matter any new military

dictator of Argentina if the Peronists have been ousted by the time this reaches print), aware of the fall of Marxist Allende of Chile, will have to devise ways of placating this extensive, educated, articulate and politically powerful group. Even the mestizo-dominated revolutionary government of Peru will fall if it does not satisfy the formerly tiny but ever more powerful middle class, which is just beginning to realize that, if Velasco is to accomplish all that he promises for the Indians of Peru, the taxes are going to have to be squeezed out of the middle class. The fact that the leaders of the Peruvian revolution are themselves mestizos will not help them, for it is their own relatives and *compadres* who will most feel the squeeze ("mestizo" used in the sense of a person of mixed white and Indian ancestry).

Northward, there is another element to be faced, that of the largely illiterate, economically stagnant but numerous mass of Indians and lower-class mestizos, mostly peasants or lumpen-proletariat, who will become increasingly politically active as farm work is more and more mechanized and no nonfarm jobs are created for them. Even rudimentary public health measures have served to cut sharply into the infant mortality rate of this segment of the population; given the always high birthrate, the fact that "the babies aren't dying like they used to" is a grim if cruel-sounding fact of socioeconomic life in all these countries (notably Bolivia, Peru and Ecuador, but including Paraguay, Colombia, and Venezuela). No return to yesterday's feudalism is possible, but neither is any extensive and extended public welfare program that would maintain this population in nonproductive idleness: the economies of these countries simply could not sustain any such effort. Education, homesteading, forced labor: these are some of the solutions proposed, but they all require a national will to solve a national problem; up to now, this has been lacking.

In Colombia particularly there seems to be a paralysis of the national will. The small coffee farmer (Juan Valdez) goes ever deeper into debt awaiting the half-smile of El Exigente; a few aging and lackluster politicians scrabble for control of a mori-

bund economy and dead political system. Sporadic and seemingly pointless violence kills a few policemen and causes leaks in a
few pipelines. Half the area of the country, the *llanos* (flatlands,
plains), ideal for cattle-raising, are two-thirds unused for in-
scrutable reasons, while mestizo cowboys butcher Indians instead of herding their stringy range cattle. In the self-styled
Athens of America (Bogotá) the people huddle in their houses
awaiting an event that does not happen. All in all, the country
seems still numbed from the effects of *la violencia,* a ten-year
(1948-58) time of widespread but mindless killing that took at
least 200,000 lives for no known cause. It is inconceivable that
this national stupor can long continue; some sort of reaction
must occur, a new leader emerge, something.

Colombia's neighbor to the east shares many of Colombia's
problems: an underdeveloped hinterland; excessive dependence
on one single export product (coffee for Columbia, oil for Venezuela); massive unemployment (which is aggravated in Venezuela's case by the fact that half a million Colombians live in
Venezuela and take jobs that could be filled by Venezuelans);
both countries have aging ex-dictators who want to come back
to power (and may have done so by the time this sees print),
and mindless terrorism. The apparent impotency of the "demo-
cratic" governments that succeeded the dictators (impotency to
solve economic problems or put down thugs masquerading as
idealists) has made it not unlikely that the dictators will come
back to office as elected presidents, unless death or senility take
their timely toll. The two countries also share a border dispute
(see Chapter Three) over oil deposits in the Gulf of Venezuela.

Venezuela, like Colombia, has underdeveloped *llanos,* but,
unlike Colombia, it also has the Guiana (or Guayana) Highlands, a vast plain of about 175,000 square miles (half the total
area of the country) at about 5,000 feet above sea level, a fertile
and mineral-rich region with an enormous hydroelectric potential. Virtually unknown until the 1930s, this region (which despite its great size holds only 3% of the country's population) is
being developed as intensively as any region in South America;
this development is not directed at a single product, but covers

iron and other mining, steel production, transportation, natural gas, agriculture, manufacturing, municipal planning (especially Cuidad Guayana, formerly Santo Tomé de Guayana), etc. This high plain extends into Venezuela's eastern neighbor Guyana (formerly British Guiana), and there are extensive Venezuelan claims to most of Guyana (see Chapter Three).

Another aspect of internal difficulties within the Spanish-speaking countries is what appears to be the failure of Marxism, in Chile and Peru. While it may be justifiably said that it is too early to declare that the experiment has failed, at least in Peru, it is certainly not too early to say that in neither case has the application of Marxist or quasi-Marxist techniques been the panacea that radical Latin Americans had for years supposed it would be. The burden of the radical song had for decades been that all the poverty and other ills of Latin America were the fault of the oligarchies and the foreign investors, and once their power were removed, the troubles would be over. But such was not the case in Peru and Chile; shortages, unemployment, inflation, poverty and strikes are still there in Peru, and socialism and Allende are both gone from Chile.

All in all, then, it must be admitted that the creation of a Spanish-speaking block in South America (with or without Argentina) is not an easy matter.

SEVEN

Some Common Factors

Any realistic viewer of Spanish South America must, taking all things into account, reach the conclusion that unifying these nations is not going to be an easy task, if indeed it is to be done at all. Squabbles among themselves, internal problems, the failures of touted panaceas all conspire to make the prospect doubtful (see previous chapter). But all hope need not be abandoned: there *are* unifying factors.

The first and foremost similarity is the common language, the second a shared attitude toward the Church. This latter phenomenon is symptomatic of other attitudes: there is reverence for the Church as the mystical body of Christ, although the phrase is never used, but hostility toward the Church as a landowning, politically and economically powerful body; as a mystical body, the Church is a tried and true teacher of humility to women and serves as the keeper of the flame of feminine chastity and eventual personal salvation for men *and* women. The opportunities for women to sin are many, but the only real sin for the men is a public display of cowardice. This common moral attitude is "common" only to the whites and upper-class and middle-class mestizos, and infects (or infuses) the Indian and lower-class mestizo masses and the blacks and mulattos only when they live in close contact with the others, but this is happening more and more, so that, in this at least, there may be a true Latin American type.

However, the general cynicism with which the worldly Church is regarded, and the lack of surprise at priestly venality or lechery or greed, carries over to other institutions; Spanish-speaking South Americans seem to share a general lack of faith in their sociopolitical institutions. Legislators, judges, presidents, governors, civil servants, in fact all men in positions of public trust are *assumed* to be venal and self-interested. An occasional individual man may become a hero (as Perón was to many in Argentina) but this does not enhance the office he holds; it merely means that he is an unusual man in that he has not devoted all of his efforts to improving his own (and his family's) position.

In the opinion of this observer, there are only two institutions which have escaped the cynicism with which all other institutions are regarded. One is the extended family, and the other is the military establishment.

The extended family includes blood relations, but also intertwines with other blood-related groups by a complicated system of intermarriage and compadrazgo (the relationship between a child's natural parents and its godfather and godmother, and between the latter and the child, and among the families so united). Extended families extend throughout nations and cross frontiers. Members may have never seen or heard of each other but will help each other if possible, or will automatically give preference to one who is a member of the family group over one who is not. Regionalism, a much discussed phenomenon of the Spanish-speaking world, is probably an historical extension of the extended family group, since anyone born in, say, Arequipa, Peru, is probably in some sort of extended-family group relationship with everyone else from that same area. When people from different regions come together on neutral ground (usually the capital or some other big city), they tend to favor their own. When two Peruvians meet for the first time, there instantly ensues a ritual verbal dance where each finds out who the other one really is, that is to say, to which extended-family groups does he belong, and whether there is any relationship between the two; more than likely there is. Something of the same sort goes on when Latin Americans from different countries first meet (again, this is more widespread among whites and acculturized mestizos than among Indians and blacks; also, the Italians of Argentina have not yet entirely worked their way into this system). It is not inconceivable that the extended family-group concept, which is a gut-felt and very serious aspect of South American society, could be a unifying factor in Spanish-speaking South America. Plans to make travel within the Andean Group easier and cheaper might, if effective, further internationalize family groups.

The other untarnished institution is the military establishment. South Americans do not really believe that soldiers are, because of their ancient and honorable profession of arms, necessarily less venal; there is something more to it than that. The writer has concluded that the high esteem in which the military is held is due to the fact that in their profession courage is the essence: a cowardly soldier is a contradiction in terms, and in South America, courage is the only true male virtue, and cowardice perhaps the only sin of which a male is capable. Thus, the military is the embodiment of virtue and the antithesis of sin. An individual officer may turn out to be a coward, but the institution cannot, and so is sacrosanct. Certainly, a military man may take a bribe, but so would a congressman or a judge; the military man is held in higher regard because he is *by profession* a man of courage. The sacrosanctity of the military may prove a powerful unifying factor.

This is even more the case if one remembers that almost the only real way that a mestizo or mulatto male can become a caballero is by becoming an officer in the armed service. It is possible that this means of social mobility will also extend to Italo-Argentines and other sons of non-Iberian Europeans. The definition of caballero in Latin America is of course impossible to state exactly, but it implies much more than the term "gentleman" as used in the United States, which seems to mean a man who does not work with his hands and opens doors for women. The Latin American caballero rarely works with his hands, must never demonstrate fear, opens doors for ladies, not women, and is conscious of his honor and is under moral obligation of reacting immediately to any slight impugning it (such slights generally involve matters relating to the chastity of his womenfolk or his own personal courage). But there is more to it than that: it is a matter of social class. Most Latin Americans of pure Iberian descent are born caballeros, and can do nothing about it one way or the other; they could not renounce the condition even if it ever occurred to them to do so. If such a one took a job working with his hands, ran away from challenges, introduced non-ladies into his society, or did any or all of the things caballeros are not supposed to do, it would not relieve him of his heritage; people would merely wonder why the caballero was acting in such a strange way. On the other hand, no mestizo or mulatto or even a white male born of non-Iberian forebears (and certainly not an Indian or black) can become a caballero except by becoming a military officer; even a rich mestizo with lackeys and a white wife will live and die a caballero *de mohatra* (a man who pretends to be a caballero without being one). But even as in medieval Spain, there exists a way that a non-caballero can *armarse caballero* (roughly, be knighted). This is by becoming a military officer. There are other avenues of social advancement, as the priesthood, the law, medicine, managerial positions, owning one's own business, but these lead to middle-class status, not to knighthood, except of course if a person was born a caballero, in which case it makes no difference what his job is.

In general, one may divide South American society into three levels: caballeros, the middle class, and the workers. The first are mainly whites and mestizos, the second mestizos or mulattos, and the third lower-class mestizos and mulattos, and Indians and blacks. While it cannot be said that everyone consciously aspires to be a caballero, it is an almost universal desideratum. Even the most radical of the revolutionary groups organize themselves along paramilitary lines; they may proclaim that they are working, fighting, robbing, kidnapping for the benefit of the poor oppressed workers, but the revolutionaries themselves see themselves as military men, thus caballeros (Fidel Castro of Cuba, even today, 14 years after his revolution, still wears battle fatigues to show that he is really a soldier, not a lawyer or a politician).

Up to now, when we have spoken of the military, we have referred especially to officers, not to the enlisted men who of course will have to do most of the fighting, if there are to be wars in Latin America. Can these men, mostly Indians and blacks and lower-class mestizos and mulattos, realistically aspire to become officers? And if the answer is negative except in the case of the smartest of them, what incentive will they have in joining the armed forces in inferior positions?

First of all, of course, they can be compelled to join by being drafted, but that is never enough. There must be real reasons to accept military service beyond the draft (and usually beyond patriotism). And ever increasingly, for the young lower-class Latin American, the armed services will be able to offer substantial advantages over civilian life. First of all, the lower-class mestizo, Indian or black is often a man without a place; where his father or grandfather had been established on a hacienda, with a place to live and a guaranteed (if humble) lifetime job and enough to eat, the new young men have either been born as unskilled laborers in a city to which their fathers had drifted, or are themselves drifting away from the hacienda for a variety of reasons (replacement by agricultural machinery, a yearning to see the city, or whatever). The armed forces can give such a man a place, feed him, give him a job, perhaps a skill, steady pay, a position, the promise of a pension, teach him pride instead of humility, teach him to read, teach him to speak Spanish as opposed to his native Indian language, in short Latinize him. And the armed forces may be the *only* place he can find these things. There is also the possibility of promotion to the noncommissioned ranks and the chance that his son can be an officer.

This view of the armed forces as the incarnation of courage and a pathway to nobility is common to all of Spanish-speaking South America, can be a unifying factor among the various nations, and should certainly ease the transition of a society traditionally based on exporting agricultural and mining products into something quite different, the shape of which cannot yet be clearly seen.

The adulation of the caballero who is also a professional military officer combines with another possibly unifying factor among Spanish-speaking South Americans: the tradition of the caudillo; most South American leaders up to now have been national figures, but it is not inconceivable that there arise a single figure capable of leading a coalition of several nations. It is predictable that, if such a one is to be found, he will be found in the officer corps. There has been one such great figure, José de San Martín, a contemporary of Bolívar's; while Bolívar is said to have liberated northern South America, San Martín liberated the southern portion of the continent; while Bolívar, a man of letters, has had many detractors, San Martín, a professional soldier, has had none. Comes there such another?

EIGHT

The Advantages of War

Professor Quincy Wright correctly perceives that, unlike science and technology, which have tended toward the continuous civilization of man, war produces great oscillations, it intensifies social cohesion within the fighting group and stimulates economic activity; while this quotation is out of context and perhaps does not fairly represent Professor Wright's ultimate conclusions, the correctness of the statements cannot be gainsaid.

The economic backwardness of the nations of South America vis-à-vis the United States and Canada, also former colonies in America, measured by per capita income or any other measuring stick, is a plain and galling fact that is self-evident to South Americans. Whatever may be the reasons (see Chapter Four), it is intolerable, and every possible action to end it *must* be taken by the leaders of South America. The highest per capita income in South America is under $900, the lowest $200; the U.S. is $4,400 and Canada well over $3,000. Nor do these figures reflect the abject poverty of the majority of South Americans, poverty undreamed of by even the poorest Americans and Canadians. Nor is this poverty any longer alleviated by the fact that the poor people are mostly peasants living on the land, where at least they have enough to eat; the well-fed if poor and humble peasantry is becoming an angry, hungry lumpenproletariat which must be pacified if chaos is to be averted.

One need not suppose that the leaders of South America, whether criollos of the oligarchy or mestizos of the middle class, will suddenly metamorphose into altruistic beings determined at last, after centuries, to improve the lot of the lower class. It is that the relentless pressure of hunger and lack of possessions combined with the first and secondhand witnessing of affluence (directly or on television and the movies) will make action in-

evitable. If the affluent flee the countries, others will take their
places; but sooner or later (and probably sooner than later)
something will have to be done.

The question then is, what *can* be done?

Many things have been tried; one of them is begging from
the rich nations; this has brought little in real wealth, and what
little came as foreign aid was usually in the first place scooped
up by the ruling oligarchy and in the second place ultimately
designed to benefit the donor, as is only right and proper, since
it is no business of the American or Russian taxpayer to take
care of South Americans. In any event, the sources are drying up
(see Chapter Two). Playing the capitalist countries off against
the socialist countries has been tried (notably by Castro in
Cuba) but this technique will become a thing of the past as
détente is reached. Local production in lieu of importation has
been tried, but with scant success since the internal market is
mostly so small that production costs are too high and it comes
out cheaper to import, which only serves to make more important the one or two export products on which the nation's economy depends.

Nor is it possible to talk about technological and scientific lack
of knowledge; in the real world, there are no secrets of this
nature. There is no doubt that Brazil could fabricate an atom
bomb tomorrow (if it has not already done so). The knowledge
is there; there is no secret about building an automobile, or a
million of them (Brazil proved that); the secret lies elsewhere:
the creation of a market, perhaps; the breaking down of the
barriers of the mind that say that the lower classes do not own
automobiles; the creation of an idea of national purpose.

Probably most important of all: the eventual realization that
the blame of South American poverty lies in South America, not
in Washington or Moscow; the final acceptance of the idea that
South America's problems must be solved in South America and
by South Americans.

Once this is believed, the first reaction will probably be to
redistribute the wealth within the country: that is to say, if it
is impossible (beyond a little expropriating) to get money from

the foreigners, then let it be gotten from the local oligarchies. This will lead to Marxist experiments, but it will inevitably be found that the oligarchy doesn't have enough to make any real dent in the poverty if it is redistributed (anyway, that portion of their wealth that the oligarchs haven't already stashed away in Swiss Banks).

As deteriorating situations oblige the only institution with any degree of popular respect (the armed forces) to take over, they will find the same problems; no longer will a few shootings and a little torture suffice. The country will have to be shaken out of its rut, that is to say, in Professor Wright's words, a great oscillation must occur, in the sense of a great swing in one direction, toward cohesion of the society and stimulation of the economy.

The only immediate way to achieve this (if not the *only* way) is war. War can give a national purpose, it can make people willing to sacrifice, to put off long-term wants to achieve an immediate end; it can employ the growing lumpenproletariat; it can justify forced migrations of peasantry back to the land to raise the needed food supply; it can satisfy the accepted cultural goals of courage; it can present an immediate enemy who can be blamed for current evils (instead of the faraway American or Russian devil). It can offer hope of victory, and then the good life to follow. It can offer the hope of alliances with neighboring nations, thus lessening the squabblings which have plagued past attempts at customs unions, even of more impressive attempts such as the Andean Group. It will make the development of domestic technology a necessity instead of a theoretical possibility.

Above and beyond these things that it can do, war is the only realistic way to avert chaos in South America in the last quarter of the twentieth century. This may seem paradoxical since war is often perceived as a chaotic endeavor, but essentially that perception is false. War, if generally accepted by the people, unifies and imposes order and discipline. True, the destruction brought on by war may sometimes so damage a nation that it never again rises (as Carthage), but mostly even the most soundly defeated nations rise again, stronger than ever (as Ger-

many and Japan after World War II). But even at the risk of complete defeat, it is hard to see what alternatives are open to the nations of South America.

Naturally, there are many things that could be done to achieve prosperity without war in South America, such as scientific agricultural planning, a cessation of class struggle, the prevalence of generalized altruism, etc., but these possibilities have always existed and have never been implemented.

NINE

Some Possible Scenarios

Across the centuries, men have not found it difficult to start wars, although the obtaining of popular backing for these endeavors has not always been as easy (witness the Vietnamese venture of the U.S.). Given the divided internal situation of most South American countries, any war would have to receive strong popular support by all sectors of the society if it is not to degenerate into civil war and a further backsliding toward chaos. Thus the leader of a South American nation who desires to lead his country into international strife will have to choose issues which are sure to generate the support of all the major factions of the society. Once such support is assured, he will be greatly aided by the fact that courage is held to be the prime virtue, since all opposition can be silenced by the accusation of cowardice. But first there must exist general support, for without that, courage could just as well be demonstrated by opposing the war, which would lead to civil war. But once the casus belli is anointed with general support, none would dare oppose it, for to do so would be to defile the national honor, which would then be an extension of one's own.

Whoever the leader is, he must therefore choose his call to arms with care. It may make little difference whether the leader actually believes in the rightness of his cause, but it is probably better if he does, since his own conviction will communicate itself to the public.

Some possible ways that wars could start in South America within a very few years are given below.

A. THE BRAZILIAN AGENTS PROVOCATEURS

Virtually every South American country except Brazil is beset by small bands of terrorists that kidnap, kill, steal, make the streets and highways unsafe, rend the internal political structure of the country, threaten (and often deliver) chaos. Such paramilitary bands have been present in countries controlled by conservatives and those controlled by Marxists, although they seem inactive in Brazil. There has been no proof whatsoever that Brazil is fostering these groups in the Spanish-speaking countries of South America, but to prove that Brazil is *not* involved is also impossible, so the lack of proof is not important. The actual terrorists themselves, mostly youngsters, may actually believe and declare (even under torture) that they are sincerely working for the good of the working classes of Argentina or Chile or Bolivia or Colombia or wherever, but they may be deluded. It used to be assumed that these bands were originally financed by Cuba or China or Russia, but why would Cuba finance a movement designed to destroy the Marxist regime of Chile? What country stands to gain by the constant internal disruption of the Spanish-speaking countries of South America? Which country wants to dominate South America? The answer to both questions, of course, is Brazil. Could Spanish-speaking Brazilian agents provocateurs be infiltrating the leftist youth of the Spanish-speaking countries, and providing money and arms and tactical know-how?

One example is the case of Argentina, Brazil's main rival for South American hegemony. The Argentine rightist military dictatorship was for years bedeviled by terrorists; finally it permitted the return of the ex-dictator Perón, the friend of the working man, and the election of a president handpicked by the aging ex-dictator; no sooner was the puppet-president Cámpora installed than the terrorism increased; a mass rally designed to welcome Perón was made a charnel house, and a rash of kidnapping ensued. Who gains by this? The Peronista party is split and may have toppled by the time this is in print; the oligarchy is being drained by ransom payments, as are foreign investors; the military, if forced to take over again, will find itself in charge of a madhouse. Argentina, in short, to the detriment of rich and worker alike, has been perhaps irretrievably weakened. Who gains? Only Brazil.

This writer is not maintaining that Brazil is in fact doing this; all that is being said here is that any clever propagandist could make an excellent logical case that this possibility exists. A little evidence (manufactured or real) would of course also be provided. The spreading of this theory throughout Spanish-speaking South America would also spread anti-Brazilian sentiment and become a unifying factor among the Spanish-speaking nations.

B. BOLIVIA PARTITIONED

A very likely event is an attempt to partition Bolivia. A possible scenario would begin with the overthrow of the government of Banzer, not an especially unlikely event in view of the fact that Bolivia has had 185 different governments in 146 years of existence. Banzer's government is a coalition of the Movimiento Nacionalista Revolucionario (MNR), which is essentially the party of the mine workers (that is to say, of the Andean part of Bolivia) and the Falange Socialista Boliviana (FSB), whose popular base of support is in the more conservative eastern or lowland part of Bolivia, especially the province of Santa Cruz. If the MNR or any leftist-dominated coalition including the MNR but excluding the FSB were to take over power, Santa Cruz (and probably the other departments of the eastern lowlands) might very possibly attempt to secede from Bolivia. These eastern lowlands constitute two-thirds of the total area of the country, but are much less heavily populated. The president, Hugo Banzer Suárez, has all the requisites of becoming a hero-leader, being a professional soldier renowned for his personal courage and honesty, acceptable to rightists and leftists, and obviously politically adept since he managed to retain the presidency for over two years in a country where the average tenure in that office is under nine months. He is also young, an important factor in a continent where old men have too much power. The exact sequence of events, and Banzer's role in them (if any), are of course impossible to foresee exactly, but it is clear that if Santa Cruz (with or without the rest of eastern Bolivia) were to secede, the question would rapidly become one of whether it would go to Brazil or to Argentina; conversely, Banzer or some other Bolivian leader might fight against the secession. The rebels would then appeal to Brazil for aid, and the central government would have to appeal to Argentina. Either way could trigger a general war involving principally Brazil and Argentina, but probably also causing the intervention of Peru as an ally of Argentina, since a Brazilian take-over of Santa Cruz brings Brazil to the eastern foothills of the Andes, something that Peru cannot want. If Peruvian troops came over the Andes to fight in Santa Cruz, while Argentine troops marched up through the Bolivian department of Tarija and so into Santa Cruz, Chile might feel uneasy at seeing her ancient enemies (Argentina, Peru and Bolivia) seemingly united. Whether Chile would in that position contemplate an alliance with Brazil by aiding the secessionists of Santa Cruz or by attacking either Argentina or Peru or both is an open question.

From the Argentine viewpoint, occupying Santa Cruz would first of all stave off Brazilian domination of that rich province, but would also in effect be a flanking movement against Paraguay, which has seemed to be drifting into the Brazilian sphere of influence. Argentina could also strike northward into Brazil through Misiones Province, which lies between the Uruguay and Paraná Rivers, in an attempt to control the enormous hydroelectric potential of these rivers, and particularly the projected Brazilian-Paraguayan dam at Itaipú on the Paraná (see Chapter Six). If this strategy were successful, Argentina would in effect hold Paraguay between the jaws of a pincer, and wrest control of it from Brazil.

Brazil of course would not be sitting still waiting for all this to happen. Allying herself with the secessionists of Santa Cruz, and if possible with Chile and above all Paraguay, Brazil could move troops into Santa Cruz, but could also (and perhaps more damagingly) drive straight south through Uruguay to face Argentina from across the River Plate.

It seems likely that if the foregoing scenario were to be followed, Venezuela would at the same time move to exert its claims on Guyana, taking advantage of Brazilian efforts to the south. Whether or not Britain would move to defend its former colony is difficult to forsee; however, whether it did or not, Argentina (now an ally of Venezuela) would occupy the Falkland Islands. If Chile were involved as an ally of Brazil, the two could attempt to squeeze Argentina out of its Antarctic claims, and the South Atlantic might be the scene of some brisk naval action.

One's best educated guess would be that Britain (and Europe and the U.S. and the U.S.S.R.) would adopt a hands-off, nonintervention policy in these wars, even if it meant the loss of the Falkland Islands and the dismemberment of the former British colony of Guyana.

As matters progressed, Brazil might eventually retaliate against Peruvian intervention by attempting to penetrate Peru's jungle province of Loreto, which would almost inevitably involve some penetration of Colombia, or at least bring Colombia into the fight to forestall such penetration. Ecuador, like Chile, would then see itself in danger of being squeezed out of existence by its traditional enemies Peru and Colombia, which would tend to bring it into the Brazilian camp. The prize in this general area of rain forest is of course oil, and Ecuador might reasonably feel that an alliance with Brazil and the possibility of recouping some land from Peru and Colombia in return for oil concessions to Brazil would be advantageous.

Given the vastness of the terrain involved, and the rather limited utility of airpower over jungles and open terrain, these wars could continue during a period of years or even decades, with armistices, provisional treaties, and periodic renewals of fighting. To what extent the belligerents could supply themselves with material, and to what extent they would have to import weapons, is an open question. Also, in this regard, to the extent that they have to import weapons, they will have to continue exporting raw materials in order to be able to pay for the imports. This opens up the possibility of attempts at blockading (as for instance a Brazilian fleet trying to close the mouth of the Plate to prevent Argentina from shipping meat or grain to

Europe, or Brazilian bombing of Venezuela's oilfields). The major nations would probably not allow interference with their own ships on the high seas, but would probably not interfere with, say, Argentine sinkings of Brazilian ships carrying coffee to New Orleans. A possible side effect of blockades and shortages of the raw materials being exported would be higher prices, so that exporting countries might get higher prices which would compensate for reduced quantities.

An immediate side effect would have to be the production in each country of sufficient food to feed itself in order not to have to import food; another effect would be a drive to industrialize so as to be able to manufacture the weapons at home instead of importing them. And a factory that makes a tank can someday make a tractor.

The foregoing scenario cannot of course be exact, but it strikes this observer as likely that the main elements of the South American wars of the last quarter of the twentieth century will be as predicted above. The main struggle will be between Brazil on the one side and Argentina and Venezuela on the other, with Colombia and Peru allied with the latter. On the west coast, Chile and Ecuador will more or less be forced to side with Brazil, or be conquered by Peru, Argentina and Colombia. Bolivia, Paraguay and Uruguay will be involved, but they may turn out to be more battlegrounds than participants. The Guianas will fall one way or the other, and be divided between Brazil and Venezuela. Naval action will occur between Argentina and Brazil in the South Atlantic, and between Chile and Peru in the South Pacific, and possibly among all four in Antarctica and the Cape Horn area. Air power will probably be directed against troops and strategic objectives such as dams and oil refineries; since this will be *una guerra entre caballeros* (a war among caballeros), there might well be a tacit agreement not to bomb each other's cities or civilian populations.

The question of who will win, if anybody wins wars, is difficult; all sorts of leaders may arise, all sorts of fighting spirit may be triggered; new alliances may form and dissolve, new confederations be created. But in general, it appears reasonable to suppose that the gifts of history (Chapter Three) will be the main bones of contention. Within a general context of Spanish versus Portuguese, Chile will still fight Peru, stronger neighbors will still try to divide Ecuador, etc. It is safe to predict that if Brazil is generally victorious, Bolivia will be divided between Brazil and Chile, and Paraguay and Uruguay will be in one way or another absorbed into Brazil's sphere of influence; Ecuador will be bigger than now, but with firm commitments to supply oil to Brazil. The Guianas will be Brazil's, and Peru will be very precariously located between larger and stronger Chile and Ecuador. Argentina will be deprived of hydroelectric power, stripped of its claims to Antarctica, and lose Misiones Province. If the other side wins, Bolivia will be divided between Argentina and Peru, Chile will be disarmed and economically absorbed by the Andean Group, Ecuador will disappear between Colombia and Peru, and Venezuela will take the Guianas. Chile and Brazil will lose their claims in Antarctica, and Uruguay and Paraguay will in effect be Argentine colonies. On the other hand, neither side may score a final victory, and the wars may end in a stalemate with some minor border changes to show that everybody won.

But whatever the political outcome, the continent as a whole should be able to feed and clothe itself, and provide itself with most of the machines it needs; no longer will it need to depend on the U.S., Europe, Russia or Japan; no longer will South America be a gaggle of comic-opera beggar nations.

Index